Bean Bag Toys

Easy-to-make Clothing, Furniture, and Accessories

Kathryn Severns

KRAUSE PUBLICATIONS

700 East State St., Iola, WI 54990-0001
Telephone (715) 445-2214
www.krause.com

Please call or write for our free catalog of publications. Our toll-free number to place an order or obtain a free catalog is 800-258-0929 or please use our regular business telephone 715-445-2214 for editorial comment and further information.

Library of Congress Catalog Number 99-60504
ISBN 0-87341-796-8

Ty and Beanie Baby are registered trademarks of Ty, Inc.; Floppy Friends is a copyright of GMA Accessories, Inc.; Home Buddies is a trademark of Russ Berrie and Co., Inc.; Precious Plush is a 1998 copyright of Anco Merchandise Co., Ltd.; Beanie Boppers, the 24K Company, and Special Effects are a trademark of Mighty Star, Inc. and 1997 copyright and trademark by DCN Industries, Inc.; Bean Sprouts is a trademark of Gift Innovations; FolkArt is a registered trademark of Plaid Enterprises, Inc.; Ceramcoat is a registered trademark of Delta Technical Coatings, Inc.; SculpeyIII is a registered trademark of Polyform Products; Velcro is a registered trademark of Velcro USA, Inc.; Styrofoam is a registered trademark of Dow Chemical, Inc.; Aleene's Original Tacky Glue is a registered trademark of Duncan Enterprises.

Acknowledgments

It is important to give credit where credit is due, and there are several people I would like to acknowledge. First and foremost, thank you to my sister Barbara Severns Czerniak and her daughter Suzanne whose clever birthday gift of outfits for my bean bag toys was the inspiration for this book. Also, thank you Barbara for the imaginative outfits you designed for this book and for the time you spent gathering materials and writing and revising directions to make sure readers could re-create your wonderful projects.

A special thank you to Eleanor Levie for suggesting I submit this book for publication and whose encouragement has helped me blossom as both a designer and writer. Thank you Mary Jo Kewley and Amy Tincher-Durik at Krause Publications for being totally enthusiastic about my ideas and to my career coach Rachelle Disbennett-Lee who has had faith in me, my talent, and my goals.

And last, but not least, thanks to four very special friends: Eileen Ramsey whose wonderful photos grace these pages, Barbara Sheehan Zeidler who listens and makes great suggestions when I bounce ideas off of her, Jackie Turner whose encouragement, editorial suggestions, and help (especially painting backgrounds and helping me write directions when I was in a pinch) are greatly appreciated, and to Pat Weeks whose wise counsel over the years has constantly guided me in the direction of my dreams.

Table of Contents

Introduction

Soft and squishy. Cute and cuddly. Bean bag toys have come a long way from the lumpy, simplistic animals my mom sewed for me when I was a child. Now they come in all shapes and sizes, and some, like Beanie Babies, are enormously popular around the world.

I have always been attracted to small stuffed toys. Their petite stature and cute features—especially their faces—make me want to

scoop them up and take them home with me. However, I must admit I was initially baffled by all of the hoopla surrounding Beanie Babies. Yes, they are cute, but so are lots of other bean bag toys. As new Beanies were introduced, there were some I was so taken with that I absolutely had to have them, and my collection of Beanies continues to grow. But the same is true of my collection of other bean bag toys. I buy the toys because I like them, not because I'm a collector. Some of my favorites have come from discount stores, pharmacies, and toy shops.

Family and friends know I collect moose, and last year my sister Barbara and my niece Suzanne gave me "Chocolate" the Beanie Baby Moose for

Bean bag toys come in a wide variety of shapes and sizes and are made by many different manufacturers. You can find them for sale in toy stores, pharmacies, gift shops, department stores, at tag sales, and on the Internet.

my birthday. A friend had already given me "Chocolate" so my sister decided to come up with a way to keep them separate. She and Suzanne created darling his and her outfits for them. Suddenly I wanted to buy and dress every bean bag toy in sight. That was how I began designing clothes and accessories for bean bag toys.

I have nothing against those people who collect bean bag toys as an investment and hope to make a fortune. Go for it! But this book is not for them; it's for those of us who buy our bean bag toys because they're cute and we want to dress them up, throw a party, and *play* with them.

Inside you'll find projects and party ideas for your bean bag toys—regardless of the kind you have. But above all, this book is about imagination, creativity, and having fun at any age. I hope you enjoy it.

Kathryn Severns

Before You Get Started

The projects in this book show you how to make a variety of clothes, costumes, and accessories for your bean bag toys. Materials needed can be purchased from your local craft or fabric store; however, I've also tried to utilize many materials which can be readily found around the house. As you gather materials, use your imagination and you're sure to come up with ideas for additional projects you can make from oatmeal boxes, paper towel rolls, fabric, and other craft supplies.

When possible, the directions include a list of the actual products used in each project. Due to changing craft trends, some products listed may not be available. However, there are sure to be substitutes which will work just as well. Don't be afraid to experiment and see what works.

This book assumes two things: one, that you have an understanding of sewing basics, and two, that you have a sewing machine. If you do not, refer to the glossary in this book for definitions of sewing terms and find a sewing machine to use, which does not need to be elaborate because you only need to do simple stitches. All of the seams in the projects are 1/8" unless otherwise noted. Most projects do not have a full hem, but if you desire a hem, adjust the pattern by adding an appropriate hem allowance.

Supplies for projects in this book can be purchased at craft and fabric stores. However, you may find you already have materials needed, such as milk cartons, paper towel rolls, and fabric, at home.

Because bean bag toys come in many shapes and sizes, the patterns used here may need to be adjusted to fit your particular toy. All of the bean bag toys used in this book measured between 8" and 9", the standard size of most bean bag toys, and the outfits are scaled to that size range. Also, the outfits were designed for toys with arms and legs and therefore may not work on toys like birds, fish, crabs, snakes, or worms.

The waist measurement on toys can vary widely depending on the number of "beans" used to fill the toy. To accommodate this, some directions will ask you to measure the waist of your toy and cut the fabric or lace used to that measurement. On other outfits, the pattern has been created to allow generous overlap and eliminate the need for adjustment. Should you have any doubt as to whether a pattern will fit your toy or not, take the toy's measurements and compare it to the pattern's measurements. You may have to enlarge or reduce the pattern to fit your particular toy.

Finally, to ensure the best possible outcome and for safety reasons, be sure to follow manufacturer's instructions and product guidelines on all products used.

Now, let's get started!

Chapter 1

Ballerina Birthday Party

As a child, I loved to pretend I was a ballerina. Inspired by their graceful movements and beautiful costumes, I would put on music and leap and twirl around the family room, creating my own "ballet." A stuffed animal was my dance partner and it would perform spectacular jumps and leaps as I tossed it into the air. At the end of our performance, we would curtsey to an adoring imaginary crowd and pick up the flowers they had thrown on stage.

In reality, I was never interested in the hours of training and practice it took to be a good dancer. Make-believe was so much more fun because I could be a famous ballerina instantly. I was content with pretending and my stuffed animal seemed to enjoy our antics as well—the smile never left its face.

Is there an aspiring young dancer in your family? Consider having a ballerina birthday party. Decorate the birthday cake with a plastic ballerina and pink icing roses. Of course, the birthday girl needs a tiara, just like a real ballerina. (The one shown in the picture came from a party store and says "Happy Birthday.") After cake and presents, clear a space and let party guests practice their pirouettes!

Activities

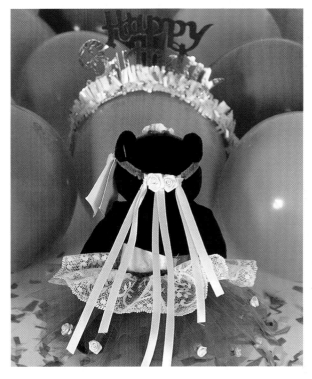

• If you live in a metropolitan area, see if a local dance troupe will let you attend a rehearsal. Little ballerinas are sure to get a kick out of watching.

• If your child's birthday is in November or December, consider taking him or her and a friend to a performance of *The Nutcracker.*

• Play classical music and let party guests dance to the music. If you've got a video camera, be sure to tape their performance!

• Present the birthday girl with a bouquet of flowers like ballerinas receive after a performance. The bouquet doesn't need to be expensive—flowers from the back yard will work just fine.

Left and above: Our beautiful ballerina is ready to perform her birthday ballet for you. After making her outfit, the two of you can practice your pirouettes. The skirt is made of emerald green tulle and is decorated with pink ribbon roses. The bodice is made from pink satin taffeta. Notice the pretty ribbon streamers on the back of her tiara. The ribbon roses, like the ones used on the tulle skirt, hide where the ribbons are attached.

Ballerina Costume

With this delightful tutu costume and a vivid imagination, you and your bean bag toy can pretend to be beautiful ballerinas and create your own ballet troupe. The tutu bodice is made of pink satin taffeta. The skirt is made of emerald green tulle and is decorated with pink ribbon roses which match the bodice. The tiara is fashioned from a green chenille stem and is decorated with pink satin ribbons and matching ribbon roses.

Bodice

Materials

3" x 14" piece of
   pink satin taffeta
Pink thread
Two snap sets
Pins, needle, scissors,
   iron

1. With right sides together, fold fabric to create a 3" x 7" rectangle. Pin front and back pattern pieces to fabric and cut out.

2. With right sides together, pin bodice pieces together and sew 1/8" seam around bodice piece, leaving bottom unsewn. Clip curves with scissors, making sure not to cut through stitching.

3. Turn right side out. Zigzag stitch across bottom opening.

4. To make bodice back, fold one bodice back piece in half with right sides together making a 1" x 3-1/4" rectangle. Stitch 1/8" seam along long edge of fabric. Turn right side out and press. Repeat for second bodice back piece.

5. Finish one end of each bodice back piece by folding edge to inside. Stitch end closed. Both bodice back pieces should have only one finished end.

6. On right side of bodice, pin unfinished edges of bodice back pieces to bodice sides, aligning bottom edges of bodice front and back pieces. On each side, sew 1/8" seam the width of bodice back piece.

7. Place bodice on toy, overlapping bodice back pieces. Mark snap placement and sew snaps in place with pink thread.

Bodice Front
Cut 1 on doubled fabric

Bodice Back
Cut 1 on doubled fabric

Tutu

1. Measure your bean bag toy's waist.

2. With needle and white thread, sew basting stitches through bound edge of white ruffled lace.

3. Gather ruffled lace to equal waist measurement. Secure basting thread and cut.

4. Thread needle with green thread. Take one 4" tulle square and pinch center of square, bunching fabric.

5. Beginning at one end of gathered lace, tack bunched tulle fabric to bound edge of gathered lace.

6. Repeat Steps 4 and 5 with remaining tulle squares, tacking to lace at regular intervals.

7. Sew sequin trim to waistline with needle and thread. Cut excess sequin trim.

8. Wrap tutu around toy's waist and mark snap placement. Sew snap set in place.

9. With scissors, remove ribbon rose stems.

10. Using glue gun, dab glue onto back of ribbon roses and attach to tulle skirt as desired.

Tiara

1. Form circle with chenille stem, overlapping ends 1". Twist stem ends to secure in place. (Where stems overlap is the tiara's back.)

2. Cut one 10" length and two 12" lengths of pink satin ribbon.

3. Fold 10" ribbon length in half. Attach ribbon to center tiara back with half hitch knot. Attach other ribbon lengths with same knot on either side of center ribbon.

4. Glue one medium ribbon rose to center front of tiara. Glue a small rose on either side of the medium rose. Repeat on top of half hitch knots in back.

Materials

18" length of 2-1/2" wide white ruffled lace

1/2 yard green tulle, cut into eighteen 4" squares

12" green single sequin trim

Two bunches small pink ribbon roses

Green and white thread

Snap set

Needle, tape measure, glue gun, scissors

Materials

8" green chenille stem

1 yard of 1/4" pink satin ribbon

2 medium pink ribbon roses

4 small pink ribbon roses

Scissors, glue gun

A craft stick corral is the perfect place to keep your bean bag ponies safe and prevent them from escaping. In an authentic western outfit that you can make, our cowboy keeps a watchful eye on these frisky fillies.

Chapter 2

Wild West Party

O.K., pardoner, saddle up them ponies and let's ride! Who among us hasn't been fascinated by the Wild West? A party with a western theme is sure to be a hit with your little cowboys and cowgirls. Wild broncos stand ready to be tamed with love by a bean bag toy dressed in a vest, chaps, bandanna print neckerchief, and 10-gallon hat. Making a craft stick corral for bean bag horses is a quick, easy, and inexpensive party activity!

Decorations

If your party is being held outdoors, bales of hay are great, inexpensive decorations. They also make great forts if your cowboys and cowgirls decide to reenact the "Shoot-out at the O.K. Corral." Inexpensive bandanna print fabric can make a no-sew table cloth or napkins. Should you live close to a stable, borrow horseshoes as a curiosity for the kids or use them as a weight to hold down items on the table that might blow away in a breeze. Just make sure you wash them before using!

Activities and Ideas

• For a fun pre-party activity, cut out or draw pictures of horses, cowboys, boots, or other western-related items and make your own party invitations.
• Paint two cardboard boxes to look like a cow and stack them on top of each other. Make a lasso from rope and a hula hoop and let the children take turns trying to lasso the cow.
• Cattle drives and branding were extremely important in the American West because they showed the animal's ownership. Party guests can create their own brands by carving a potato and making potato print brands. Decorate goodie bags by dipping stamps in stamping ink or paint and pressing the stamp onto the bags.
• Sit around a make-believe camp fire and sing western theme songs like "Home on the Range," "Camp Town Ladies," and "Don't Fence Me In."
• Make your own sheriff's badges from cardboard and aluminum foil. Make a six-pointed star base from cardboard and cover with aluminum foil. Hot glue a pin back or safety pin onto the back of the star and deputize the entire party!
• Invite guests to come wearing western attire or have dress-up clothing available.
• If bad weather forces your gathering inside, rent an old western movie for the kids to watch.

Food

After a full day of busting broncos and roping cattle, feed your hungry little buckaroos delicious grub from your chuck wagon.

Menu

Hamburgers or cheeseburgers on toasted buns
Ketchup, mustard, mayonnaise, pickles
Baked beans
Potato salad (recipe below)
Carrot sticks and apple wedges (for people or ponies!)

Barbara's Best Potato Salad

Ingredients

(Serves eight to ten)
Six or seven large red-skinned potatoes
One stalk celery
Half of medium onion
1/2 cup real mayonnaise
1 Tbs. lemon juice
1 tsp. spicy brown mustard
Salt
Pepper
Paprika

My sister Barbara makes potato salad so delicious both kids and adults go back for seconds, even thirds! The secret: chopping celery and onion finely and letting the salad refrigerate for several hours so that the flavors meld.

1. Place whole, unpeeled potatoes in a 4-quart cooking pot, adding enough water to cover the potatoes. Bring water to boil and add 1/2 tsp. salt. Cook potatoes until just tender; do not over-cook.

2. Remove from heat and drain boiling water. Fill pot with cold water to stop potatoes from cooking further. When cool, drain water and peel potatoes, removing any eyes or blemishes.

3. Cut peeled potatoes into 1" cubes and place in a bowl. Sprinkle cut potatoes with lemon juice. Add salt and pepper to taste.

4. Finely chop onion and celery. Add to potatoes along with mayonnaise and mustard. If potato salad doesn't look "wet," add more mayonnaise, one tablespoon at a time until salad has desired consistency.

5. Sprinkle top with paprika.

6. Cover and allow to sit in the refrigerator for several hours before serving.

Wild West Outfit

This handsome cowpoke is ready to saddle up and ride. Colorful bandanna print fabric is used for the vest and neckerchief. Chaps, which protect the legs of our working cowboy, are made from vinyl. A straw 10-gallon hat, purchased at a craft store, completes the outfit.

Chaps

1. Fold two-thirds of fabric with right sides together, leaving a 5" portion of the fabric unfolded. Pin chap back to fabric, placing pattern fold line on fabric fold. Pin chap fringe pattern to doubled fabric. Pin right and left chap front patterns to unfolded fabric piece. Cut out.

2. With right sides together, sandwich fringe rectangle piece between chap front and back. Pin chap left front, fringe, and back together and sew a 1/8" seam. Repeat for right side.

3. Turn right side out. To make chap fringe, cut slits in rectangle with scissors to within 1/8" of seam.

4. Place chaps around toy, overlapping front edges, and mark snap placement.

5. Sew snap in place with needle and thread.

Materials

5" x 15" vinyl, felt, or suede-look fabric (fabric used for this project must not fray)
Snap set
Thread to match fabric
Scissors, pins, needle

Vest

Materials

9" x 12" piece of cotton fabric, preferably bandanna print
Thread to match fabric
Scissors, pins, iron

1. With right sides together, fold fabric. Pin vest front and back pieces to folded fabric, placing vest back fold line on fabric fold. Cut out.

2. Finish raw edges of vest front pieces by turning neck, vest front opening, and bottom points under 1/8" and sew.

3. Turn under vest bottom back edge 1/8" and sew.

4. With right sides together, place right and left vest front pieces on top of vest back, aligning sides and shoulders. Pin sides and shoulders. Sew with 1/8" seam.

5. At back neck opening, turn under raw edge 1/8" and topstitch with sewing machine.

6. Turn vest right side out and press.

Neckerchief

Materials

5" x 5" square piece of bandanna print fabric
Pony bead
Small safety pin or crochet hook

1. Fold fabric square along the diagonal to create a triangle.

2. With center triangle point in front of bean bag toy, wrap ends around toy's neck.

3. Using a safety pin or crochet hook, pull ends of fabric through pony bead.

4. Adjust tightness of neckerchief by sliding fabric through bead.

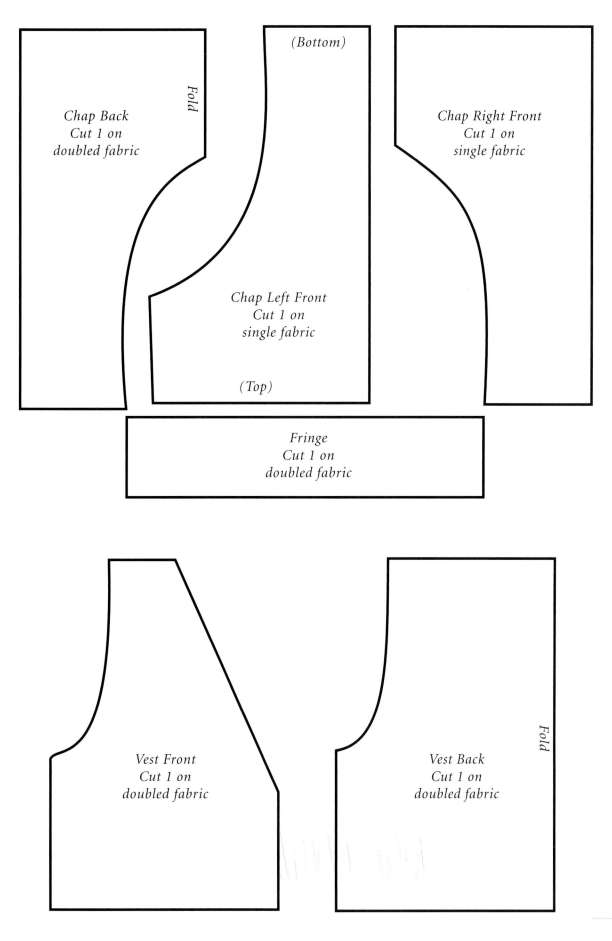

Chap Back
Cut 1 on
doubled fabric

Fold

(Bottom)

Chap Right Front
Cut 1 on
single fabric

Chap Left Front
Cut 1 on
single fabric

(Top)

Fringe
Cut 1 on
doubled fabric

Vest Front
Cut 1 on
doubled fabric

Vest Back
Cut 1 on
doubled fabric

Fold

15

Craft Stick Corral

Materials

Wooden craft sticks
Glue gun

Fig. 1

Fig. 2

Craft sticks make an inexpensive corral for your bean bag toy horses. A glue gun lets you make corral segments in a matter of minutes. However, they can be very hot, so use with caution or select a low-temperature model.

1. Create two corral fence ends by making an "X," placing one craft stick on top of another as shown.

2. Glue where sticks cross (Fig. 1).

3. At the top of the intersecting craft sticks, glue cross piece as shown (Fig. 2).

4. Glue bottom cross piece beneath the intersecting craft sticks.

5. Repeat Steps 1 through 4 to create desired number of corral fence pieces.

Chapter 3

Mexican Fiesta

No need to wait for Cinco de Mayo, Mexican Independence Day, to throw a party; any day is the perfect day for a Mexican fiesta. Dress your bean bag toys in traditional costumes—sombrero and poncho for him, Flamenco dress for her—and bring them to the party!

Decorations

A piñata makes a wonderful focal point for fun. Traditionally made from papier mâché and decorated with brightly-colored tissue paper, you can make your own or buy one at a party store. Fill the piñata with candy, party favors, or small toys and suspend it in the center of a room or outside over a tree limb. Let each guest take a turn to try and crack it open. Blindfold them, spin them around three times, and, using a broomstick or thick dowel, let them take a few swings. Just make sure there are no breakables or other children within swinging range!

Confetti made from leftover tissue paper makes decorating your table a snap. Just sprinkle it on a plastic tablecloth for instant party atmosphere. Other easy and inexpensive decorations: tissue paper flowers and Mexican travel posters from your local travel agent. (And don't forget those postcards and souvenirs from your trips south of the border!)

Our señor and señorita look sensational sitting on the branches of a saguaro cactus in outfits you can make. Tissue paper flowers and confetti add to the festive atmosphere.

Tissue Paper Flowers

Decorations for your party don't need to be expensive. Tissue paper flowers are colorful and easy to make. Depending on the age of your guests, flowers are a great craft activity which can be made and taken home.

Materials

Brightly-colored tissue paper (multicolored packs of tissue paper available at craft stores are perfect for this)
Stem wire or chenille stems
Scissors, ruler

Fig. 1

1. Stack five sheets of tissue paper.

2. Cut stacked paper into 10" widths.

3. Fold tissue paper to create 1" wide accordion pleats (Fig. 1).

4. Mark center of accordion pleats (Fig. 2).

Fig. 2

5. Fold wire or chenille stem in half and place pleated paper in the center. Twist to secure (Fig. 3).

6. Using scissors, round ends of pleated paper to create petal effect (Fig. 4).

7. Spread out folds. Carefully separate tissue paper layers and pull toward center wire (Fig. 5).

Fig. 3

8. Continue until all layers are unfolded (Fig. 6).

Fig. 6

Fig. 5

Fig. 4

Food
Quick and Easy Quesadillas

Ingredients

Flour tortillas
Grated cheese

Ingredients

Flour tortillas
Peanut butter
Jelly

Type 1

Preheat oven to 350°. Sprinkle tortilla with grated cheese. Cover with another tortilla and heat until cheese melts. Cut into wedges and serve warm.

Type 2

Spread tortilla with peanut butter and jelly. Cover with another tortilla and cut into wedges and serve.

Poncho and Sombrero
Designed by Barbara Czerniak

Our bean bag pal is ready for a day south of the border dressed in a poncho and matching sombrero. Whether walking around the town square or stopping to take a siesta after a delicious lunch, he'll look dapper in this dashing outfit.

Poncho

1. With right sides together, fold fabric to create a 3-1/2" x 9" rectangle.

2. Pin pattern to fabric, placing pattern fold line along fabric fold. Cut out. **Do not cut along fold line**.

3. With pencil, mark cutting line from poncho neck front to small dot.

4. With adhesive sides together, fold interfacing and pin interfacing pattern to iron-on interfacing, placing pattern fold line on fabric fold. Cut out.

5. With adhesive side to wrong side of fabric, place interfacing so that it matches neck opening. Iron interfacing in place.

6. Cut along cutting line to small dot through fabric and interfacing.

7. Topstitch entire neck opening including front slit. Secure threads.

8. Fold under side edges of poncho 1/4". Press and stitch.

9. Fold under front and back bottom edges 1/4". Press and topstitch along edges.

10. Measure front and back bottom edges. Cut fringe pieces to fit edges. Pin fringe to poncho 1/4" above finished edge and sew in place.

11. Place poncho on bean bag toy and mark snap or fastener placement under both arms. Sew in place with needle and thread.

Materials

7" x 9" piece of striped upholstery fabric
Small piece of iron-on interfacing
7" of 1" wide fringe
Thread to match fabric
Two snap sets or Velcro fasteners
Pins, scissors, tape measure, needle, iron, pencil

Sombrero

Materials

6" x 15" piece of striped upholstery fabric
One package 7 mm pompoms
6" of 1/8" wide elastic
Thread
Pins, scissors, glue gun, needle

1. Fold two-thirds of fabric with right sides together, leaving a 5" portion of the fabric unfolded. Place hat brim pattern on folded fabric portion and hat top on unfolded fabric.

2. Pin hat patterns to fabric and cut out.

3. With wrong sides together, pin hat brims. Sew a zigzag stitch along both inner and outer edges of hat brim.

4. With right sides of hat top together, pin and sew straight edges. Turn right side out.

5. Center hat top in middle of hat brim. Pin hat top to brim.

6. Sew hat top to brim along hat top edge, making sure to catch brim on underside.

7. Using glue gun, glue pompoms along underside edge of hat brim at even intervals.

8. Place hat on bean bag toy. Stretch elastic slightly and measure the elastic from one side of inner hat brim under toy's "chin" to other side of inner hat brim. Elastic should hold hat snugly to toy's head. Cut elastic.

9. Sew elastic in place with needle and thread.

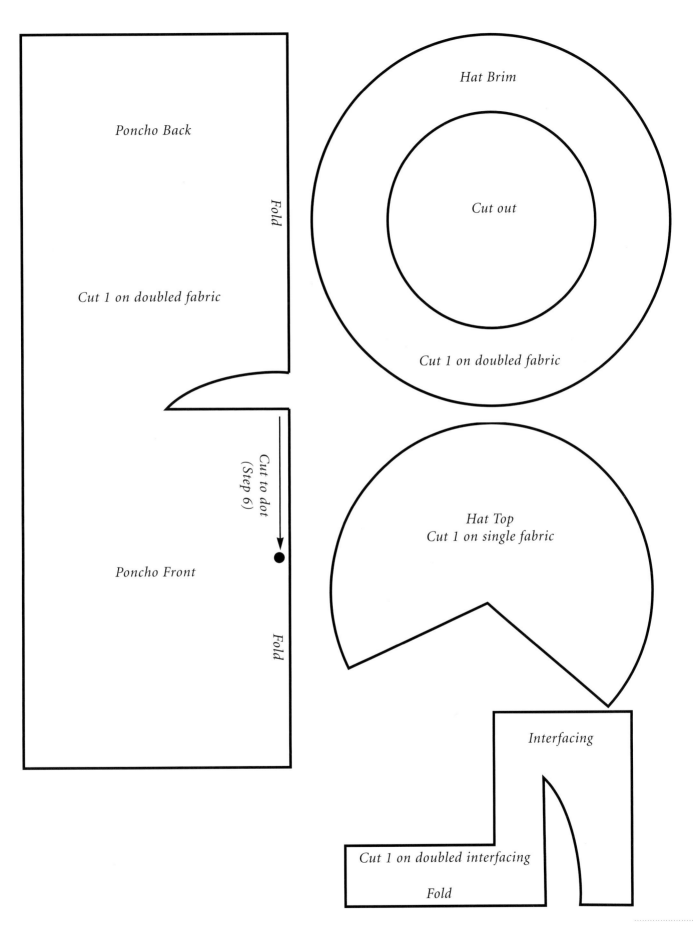

Poncho Back

Cut 1 on doubled fabric

Fold

Cut to dot
(Step 6)

Poncho Front

Fold

Hat Brim

Cut out

Cut 1 on doubled fabric

Hat Top
Cut 1 on single fabric

Interfacing

Cut 1 on doubled interfacing

Fold

Flamenco Skirt, Jacket, and Tiara

Designed by Barbara Czerniak

Our beautiful señorita is dressed in a flamenco outfit, reflecting her Spanish heritage. Wearing a lace-trimmed skirt and jacket, she's ready to go to the ball and dance the night away. Watch as she stomps her feet and sways in a traditional dance.

Skirt

1. Sew 1/4" hem along one 15" edge of fabric.

2. Cut lace into three 15" pieces.

3. To create lace tiers, on front of fabric, pin and sew one 15" lace piece along skirt's hemmed edge.

4. Pin and sew second layer of lace on fabric so bottom edge of lace covers stitching of bottom layer.

5. Pin and sew third layer of lace so bottom edge of lace covers stitching of the second tier.

6. Measure waist of bean bag toy.

7. With needle and thread, sew basting stitch along unsewn 15" side of fabric. Pull thread to gather fabric. Gathered fabric should equal waist measurement. Secure threads.

8. Fold skirt, with right sides together, pin and sew a 1/8" seam halfway up the back seam, about 2-1/4".

9. Press seam open. Press under unsewn back edges of skirt 1/8" and topstitch.

10. Measure and cut bias tape around gathered waistline, adding 1" to measurement.

11. Fold raw ends of bias tape under 1/4" and press.

12. To make waistband, beginning at back edge of skirt, fold and pin bias tape over gathered fabric. Waistband end will extend 1/2" from waist. Sew waistband in place, making sure to sew through both layers of bias tape.

13. Sew snap to waistband extension and edge of waistband with needle and thread.

Materials

5" x 15" piece of red cotton or cotton blend fabric
1-1/4 yards of gathered 1" lace
1/4 yard bias tape to match fabric
Thread to match fabric
Pins, tape measure, needle, iron

Jacket

Materials

12" x 12" piece of red cotton or cotton blend fabric
1/2 yard of gathered 1" lace
3/4 yard bias tape to match fabric
Small bow or flower
1/4 yard of gathered 1" lace
Thread to match fabric
Snap set
Tape measure, needle

1. With right sides together, fold fabric in half to create a 12" x 6" rectangle.

2. Pin jacket pattern pieces to fabric, placing back pattern's fold line on fabric fold. Cut out.

3. With right sides together, pin and sew front and back jacket pieces at shoulder.

4. Beginning at bottom front edge of jacket, measure bias tape along front edge, around neck edge, and down other front edge to bottom of jacket. Cut.

5. Fold and pin bias tape over raw edges of jacket front, starting at front bottom edge and proceeding around neck edge and down other front jacket edge.

6. Sew bias tape making sure to catch all layers of fabric.

7. Sew 1/8" seam along lower sleeve edges.

8. Measure lace along sleeve edge and cut. Repeat for other sleeve edge.

9. Place and pin bound edge of lace along inside bottom edge of sleeve. Sew lace in place along sleeve edge. Repeat for other sleeve.

10. With right sides together, pin side and sleeve seams together. Starting at jacket bottom, sew a 1/8" seam along side, pivoting at underarm and continuing to end of sleeve.

11. Cut small slit at underarm, being careful not to cut through stitching.

12. Turn right side out and press.

13. With ruffle extending out from jacket, pin lace to wrong side of jacket, beginning at front bottom edge. Continue around neck edge and down other front jacket edge. Sew with needle and thread.

14. Sew 1/8" hem along jacket bottom.

15. Place jacket on bean bag toy and mark snap placement. Sew snap in place with needle and thread.

16. Sew bow or flower on jacket front.

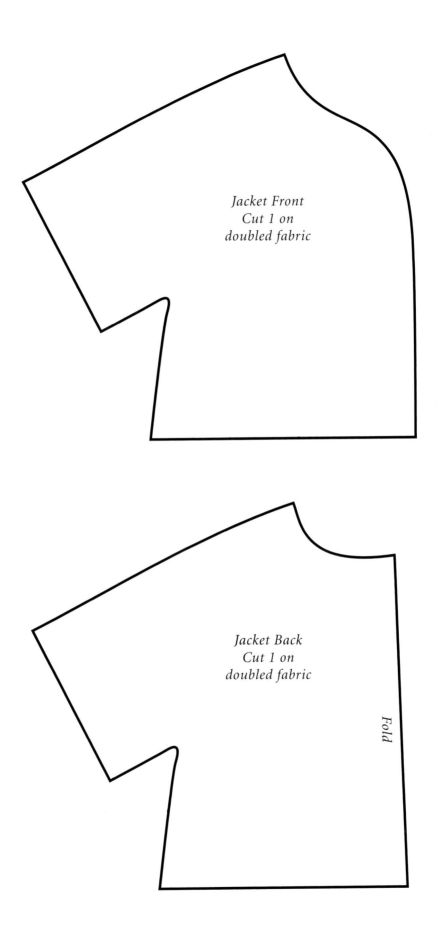

Jacket Front
Cut 1 on
doubled fabric

Jacket Back
Cut 1 on
doubled fabric

Fold

Tiara

Materials

12" of 1/8" elastic
2/3 yard bias tape to match skirt and jacket fabrics
Small bow or flower
Thread to match bias tape
Pins, small safety pin, needle, tape measure

1. Measure and cut two 10" pieces of bias tape.

2. With wrong sides of bias tape together, pin long sides together.

3. Make a tube by sewing bias tape close to edges.

4. Measure around bean bag toy's head, subtracting 1/2". Cut elastic to this length.

5. Attach elastic to small safety pin and thread through tube, making sure opposite end does not come through tube. Material will "scrunch" up along elastic.

6. Keeping materials straight, pin ends of elastic to ends of tube.

7. With right sides together, pin ends of tube together and sew.

8. Place tiara on toy's head with seam at back.

9. Mark bow or flower placement at center front of tiara. Sew in place with needle and thread.

Chapter 4

Dog Gone It!

Man's best friend is even more adorable when dressed in a vest and shorts set accented by a dog bone-shaped button. The bone button can be purchased at a sewing specialty shop or can easily be made from polymer modeling material. This same modeling material is used to make our dog bone-shaped necklace pieces, shown below, the perfect gift for any dog bean bag toy owner. A milk carton is easily converted into a great dog house—one that any pooch or puppy would be happy in!

I think you'll agree—these projects are just too dog gone cute! A dog bone-shaped button is the perfect choice to complete this vest and shorts outfit. Got milk? Then you've got the main ingredient needed to make this darling dog house—a milk carton. Corrugated paper covers the sides and a plain piece of cardboard forms the roof. Any canine would be happy to call this home!

Dog Bone Necklace

This necklace is a great gift for the owner of any dog—bean bag or real. "Bones" are first fashioned from polymer modeling material and then baked. The necklace length can be adjusted by adding or removing bones.

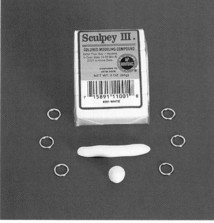

Materials

*One package white
polymer modeling
material**
Pin or thick needle
Fifty jump rings
*Baking sheet (This
sheet should not
be used for
cooking or come in
contact with food
after using to bake
modeling material.
A disposable
aluminum tray is
recommended.)*

Used in this project:
*SculpeyIII

1. Pinch off small piece of clay. Roll piece into small "snake," approximately 3/4" long and 3/8" in diameter (Fig. 1).

2. Pinch off four pieces of clay and form into four balls 3/8" in diameter. Place two balls on each end of the snake (Fig. 2).

3. Flatten, mold, and shape clay with fingers into dog bone shape so it is approximately 1-1/2" long (Figs. 3 and 4).

4. Stick pin or thick needle through center ends of bone, making hole big enough for jump ring to fit through (Fig. 5).

5. Repeat above steps to make a total of ten bones.

6. Bake clay according to manufacturer's directions.

7. Place jump ring in each dog bone end (Fig. 6).

8. Connect bones with three more jump rings (Fig. 7).

9. Continue connecting bones until circle necklace is formed.

Fig. 1

Fig. 2

Fig. 3

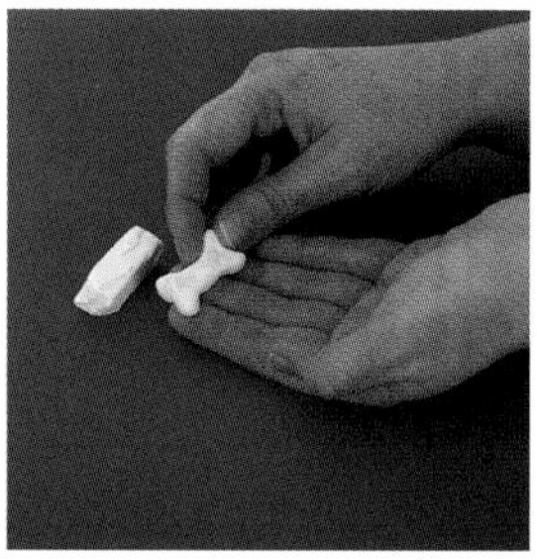

Fig. 4

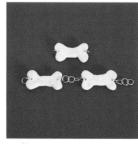

Fig. 5

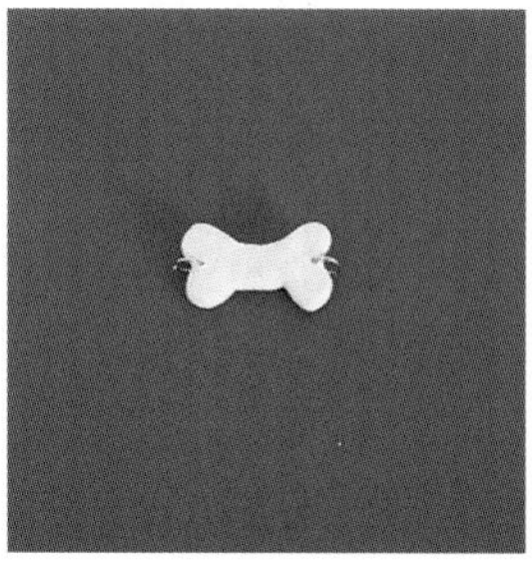

Fig. 6

Fig. 7

Dog Bone Button

Dog bone-shaped buttons are available at fabric stores, but tend to be expensive. You can make your own buttons inexpensively and easily using polymer modeling material.

Follow directions for dog bone necklace with the following exceptions:
• "Snake" should be 3/8" long and 1/4" in diameter.
• Balls should be 1/4" in diameter.
• Finished button length should be approximately 3/4".
• Stick pin or needle into center of bone, making two holes. (Make sure holes are large enough for needle and thread to pass through.)

Materials

Polymer modeling material*
Pin or thick needle
Baking sheet (This sheet should not be used for cooking or come in contact with food after using to bake modeling material. A disposable aluminum tray is recommended.)

Used in this project:
*SculpeyIII

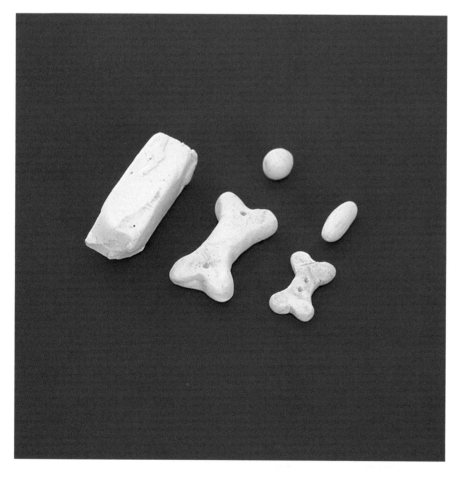

A lump of polymer molding material (left) is easily fashioned into a boned-shaped "bead" (center) or button (right).

Vest and Shorts

Any canine bean bag toy will look dog gone cute in this vest and shorts outfit made from burgundy and tan plaid fabric. The dog bone-shaped button can be purchased or made from polymer modeling material (see page 33).

Vest

Materials

6" x 9" piece of burgundy and tan plaid fabric
Thread to match fabric
Snap set
Pins, scissors, needle, iron
Dog bone button (see page 33)

1. Fold fabric to create a 3" x 9" rectangle. Pin pattern to fabric, placing pattern fold line along fabric fold. Cut out.

2. Finish raw edges by turning front vest edges under 1/8" and sew.

3. Turn vest back's bottom edge under 1/8" and sew.

4. With right sides together, place right and left vest front pieces on top of vest back, aligning sides and shoulders. Pin sides and shoulders. Sew with 1/8" seam.

5. At back neck opening, turn under raw edge 1/8" and topstitch with sewing machine.

6. Turn vest right side out and press.

7. Overlap vest fronts, marking position for snap set. Sew snaps in place with needle and thread.

8. Sew dog bone button onto front of vest, over the snaps.

Shorts

1. Fold fabric to create a 3" x 9" rectangle. Pin pattern to fabric, placing pattern fold line along fabric fold. Cut out. Repeat so you have two shorts pieces.

2. To hem leg openings, fold under bottom edge of both short pieces 1/8" and stitch.

3. With right sides together, sew a 1/8" seam along diagonal of one piece to form leg opening. Repeat for second piece.

4. Open sewn shorts sections. Beginning at waist of shorts, with right sides together, pin sections together. Sew continuous 1/8" seam from front through shorts crotch to back.

5. Fold and sew 1/4" casing at waist, leaving small opening at shorts back.

6. Measure waist of bean bag toy and subtract 1/2". Cut elastic to this measurement.

7. Pin small safety pin to elastic and thread through casing.

8. Sew ends of elastic together with needle and thread.

Materials

6" x 9" piece of burgundy and tan plaid fabric
Thread to match fabric
12" of 1/8" elastic
Pins, scissors, needle, tape measure, small safety pin

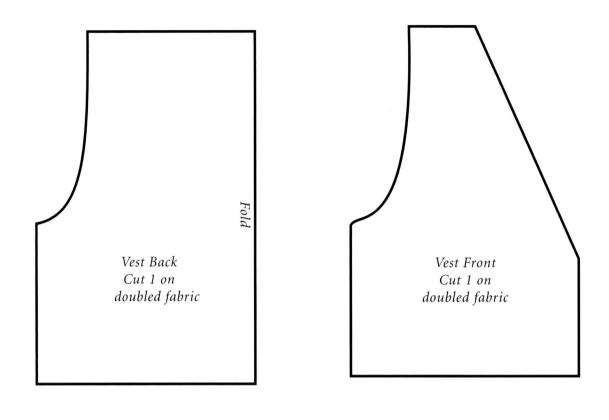

Vest Back
Cut 1 on
doubled fabric

Fold

Vest Front
Cut 1 on
doubled fabric

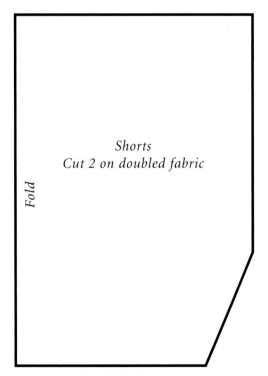

Shorts
Cut 2 on doubled fabric

Fold

Dog House

A half-gallon milk or juice carton is the base of our darling dog house. Corrugated paper resembles corrugated construction material sometimes used to make real dog houses. But, no matter what material you use to make your dog house, your canine companion is sure be happy in this home!

1. Trace dog house pattern pieces onto corrugated paper or mat board and cut out. (Note: Roof piece needs to be enlarged.)

2. Draw a line 3-1/2" from bottom edge around carton. Cut along this line and remove bottom of carton.

3. Place pointed dog house piece with door cut-out onto side where the milk carton spout opening is. Trace door opening onto carton. Cut out door.

4. Glue carton folded spout opening closed.

5. Glue door piece to carton, aligning bottom and door opening.

6. Glue second pointed dog house piece to opposite side of carton.

7. Glue square pieces to sides of carton.

8. Mark half-way point of cardboard's 8-1/2" side. Fold cardboard in half at this point and glue to top of dog house.

Materials

6" x 16" piece of corrugated paper or mat board
Half-gallon milk or juice carton (empty)
5" x 8-1/2" piece of plain cardboard
Scissors, glue gun, pencil

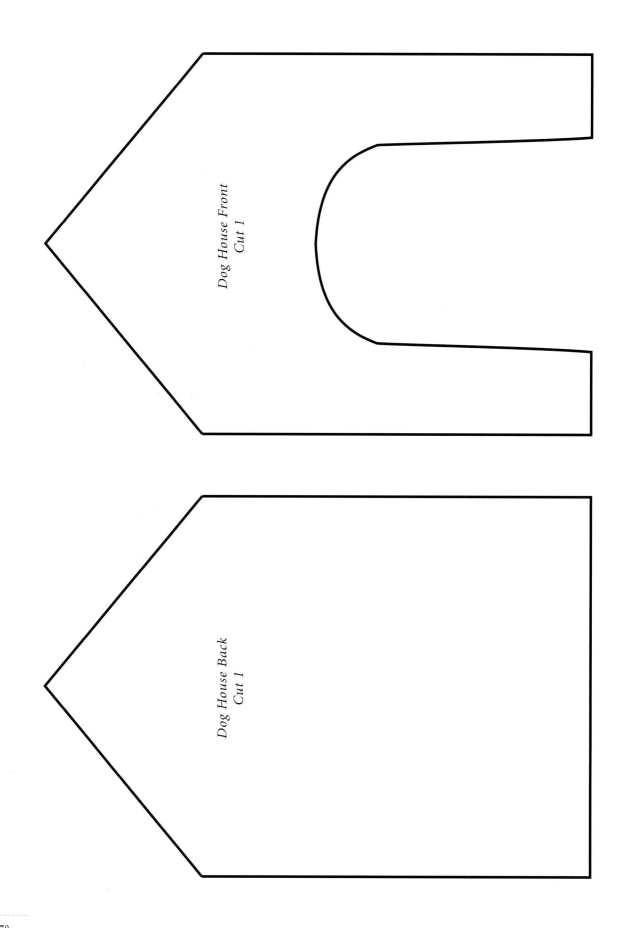

Dog House Front
Cut 1

Dog House Back
Cut 1

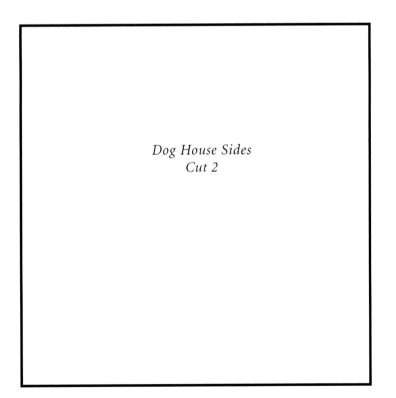

Dog House Roof   *Enlarge 200%*

Fold line

Dog House Sides
Cut 2

Chapter 5

Garden Goodness

How does your garden grow? It may not have silver bells, cockle shells, and pretty maids all in a row, but it can sport rows of pots with painted plant pokes. Wearing a sunflower print top, coordinating shorts, and hat, the raccoon bean bag toy has stopped to admire the green and gold birdhouse sitting in a terra cotta pot.

Gardening is a hobby that can become a life-long passion. Whether you live in the city, suburbs, or country, you can grow plants. Watching seeds sprout, grow, and mature is exciting and teaches us about life cycles. Eating the fruits of your labor is a delicious reward for your hard work. Store-bought vegetables just don't taste the same as those picked fresh from your garden. Little ones may discover they actually like vegetables they swear they hate!

Think a garden might be too much work? Look for a community garden or see if you can share the work and the rewards with neighbors—that way, everyone benefits. Looking for a good deed to do? Share your garden's bounty with a food bank or the elderly.

Activities

• Save your egg cartons and use them to start seeds. Remove the lid and put it underneath the carton to use as a drainage tray. If cartons are made from Styrofoam, poke holes in the bottom of the egg cups to allow soil to drain. If cartons are cardboard, line the lid tray with plastic wrap to make it water resistant. Fill the egg carton with soil and plant seeds according to seed pack directions. Be sure to water regularly and be patient. In a few days your seeds will sprout, and your garden will be on its way!

• Have a true garden party using fruits and vegetable from your garden. Make tea sandwiches with thinly-sliced vegetables and desserts from berries such as strawberries, raspberries, or black berries. Yum!

• After you've planted your garden, keep birds from eating your seeds by creating a scarecrow or another diversionary device. A quick, easy, and inexpensive device can be made from strips of aluminum foil or foil pans attached to a string and tied to garden stakes at the end of each row.

Left: This raccoon bean bag toy is waiting to see if a bird will nest in its birdhouse plant poke. Plant pokes add a decorative touch to house plants and come in a variety of shapes and sizes.

Food
Dirt Dessert

Ingredients

(Serves four to six)
One chocolate cookie
1-1/2 cups chocolate cookie crumbs
One package chocolate pudding
One package butterscotch pudding
Worm-shaped gum candies
6" clay pot

1. Wash clay pot thoroughly with dish detergent and warm water. Let dry.

2. Place chocolate cookie over drainage hole in bottom of pot.

3. Place 1" layer of chocolate cookie crumbs in the pot.

4. Make chocolate and butterscotch pudding according to package directions. Spoon 2" layer of butterscotch pudding on top of cookie crumbs.

5. Place worm candies on top of pudding. Cover with 1/2" layer of cookie crumbs.

6. Spoon 2" layer of chocolate pudding on top of cookie crumbs and worm candies.

7. Cover chocolate pudding with 1/2" layer of cookie crumbs.

Note: This dessert can be made in individual servings. Use 3" pots and layer ingredients in smaller amounts.

Shirt and Shorts

No matter what the weather is outside, the sunflower print fabric used in this outfit is sure to chase the clouds away. Your bean bag toy will enjoy a day of gardening in this comfortable shirt and shorts outfit. The shirt features grosgrain ribbon side ties. The elastic waist shorts are made from a coordinating burgundy and tan plaid fabric.

Shirt

1. With right sides together, fold fabric to create a 4-1/2" x 5" rectangle. Pin pattern to fabric, placing pattern fold line on fabric fold. Cut out.

2. Sew 1/8" hem along shirt sides, bottom, and neck opening.

3. Cut grosgrain ribbon into four 4" pieces.

4. Position shirt on toy and mark placement of ribbon ties in middle of shirt.

5. Sew ribbons in place.

6. To make shoulder ruffles, with needle and thread, sew running stitch in an arc from shoulder front to shoulder back.

7. Pull thread to gather fabric and create shoulder ruffle. Secure thread with knot.

8. Repeat Steps 6 and 7 on other side.

Shorts

1. Fold fabric to create a 3" x 9" rectangle. Pin pattern to fabric, placing pattern fold line along fabric fold. Cut out. Repeat so you have two shorts pieces.

2. To hem leg openings, fold under bottom edge of both short pieces 1/8" and stitch.

3. With right sides together, sew a 1/8" seam along diagonal of one piece to form leg opening. Repeat for second piece.

Materials

4-1/2" x 10" piece of sunflower print fabric
16" of 1/4" grosgrain ribbon
Thread to match fabric
Pins, scissors, needle

Materials

6" x 9" piece of burgundy and tan plaid fabric
Thread to match fabric
12" of 1/8" elastic
Pins, scissors, needle, small safety pin, tape measure

4. Open sewn shorts sections. Beginning at waist of shorts, with right sides together, pin sections together. Sew a continuous 1/8" seam from front through shorts crotch to back.

5. Fold and sew 1/4" casing at waist, leaving small opening at shorts back.

6. Measure waist of bean bag toy and subtract 1/2". Cut elastic to this measurement.

7. Pin small safety pin to elastic and thread through casing.

8. Sew ends of elastic together with needle and thread.

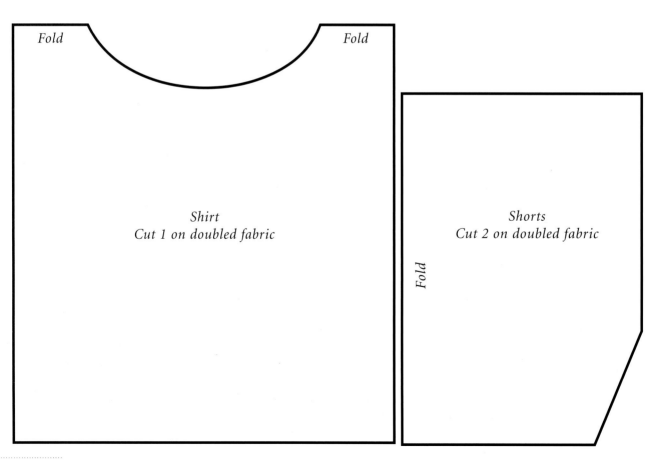

Fold   *Fold*

Shirt
Cut 1 on doubled fabric

Fold

Shorts
Cut 2 on doubled fabric

Birdhouse Plant Poke

Spruce up ordinary looking house plants with decorated plant pokes, which can be purchased at a craft store. The poke consists of a birdhouse ornament attached to a wooden dowel. Pokes can be decorated by painting with acrylic paints. Once dry, insert the painted plant poke into the dirt and change your plant from ordinary to extraordinary.

Materials

Wooden birdhouse plant poke (unfinished)
Green and gold acrylic paint*
3" terra cotta pot
Sand
Sandpaper, masking tape, paint brush, saw (optional)

Used in this project:
*Plaid Folk Art Harvest Gold and Clover acrylic paints

1. Sand plant poke's rough edges if needed.

2. Paint top half of birdhouse with green paint (Fig. 1). Use tape to mask bottom half of birdhouse front and back if desired.

3. Paint bottom half of birdhouse with gold paint (Fig. 2).

4. Place tape over hole in bottom of terra cotta pot. Fill pot with sand (Fig. 3).

5. If necessary, adjust plant poke height by sawing off excess dowel. Stick plant poke into sand.

Fig. 1

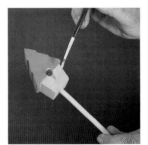

Fig. 2

Fig. 3

Chapter 6

Pirate Party

Yo, ho, ho! Let's have some fun! A pirate party is sure to be a hit. Our swashbuckling bean bag toy is outfitted in a striped shirt with belt, eye patch, and bandanna headpiece. Watch out! He's likely to steal your heart along with your jewels.

Craft projects, like the treasure box and palm trees, have been designed to require minimal adult supervision and can be adapted to suit almost any age group. Gift wrap tubes make the trunks of the tissue paper palm trees and can be used to create make-believe swords. Foil-covered chocolate coins look like gold doubloons and make wonderful prizes for games.

Even the sweetest looking youngster can be transformed into a fierce pirate with a bandanna headpiece and an eye patch made from poster board, glue, and elastic! When guests get hungry, avoid a mutiny on the high seas with Pieces of Eight Pizza and mugs of Pirate's Grog.

Decorations

Tales of pirates and buried treasure truly capture children's imagination. Why not let them help with decorating by creating their own pirate flags and stories? Supply them with colored pencils, crayons, markers, stickers, and sheets of paper and let them spin their own stories of intrigue on the high seas.

You and your bean bag toy can set sail on the high seas of imagination with this pirate galleon, outfit, and treasure box. Bury your treasure under palm trees made from gift wrap tubes and green tissue paper.

Games
Treasure Hunt

1. Cut ten slips of paper to make clues (old road maps are great for this!).

2. On nine of the slips, write directions or rhymes telling where to find the next clue.

3. On the tenth slip, write where to find the buried treasure.

4. Goodie bags make great buried treasure. Just be sure to have names on each bag so one pirate doesn't walk off with all of the loot!

Materials

*Ten slips of paper
Treats for goodie
    bags
Pencil*

Walk the Plank

Make up pirate-related questions in advance (see sample questions and answers below). The board or beach towel is the pirate ship's plank. This game is played by having contestants step onto the plank and answer a question. If they get it right they get off the plank and go back in line. If they answer incorrectly, they walk the plank and are out of the game.

Sample Questions/Answers:

1. What does a pirate say? (Yo, ho, ho!)

2. What animal often sits on a pirate's shoulder? (A parrot)

3. What symbol is on a pirate's flag? (Skull and crossbones)

4. What did the pirate in Peter Pan have on his arm instead of a hand? (A hook)

5. What do pirates dig for? (Buried treasure)

Materials

*A board or beach
    towel folded in
    half lengthwise for
    "plank"*

Food
Pieces of Eight Pizza

Ingredients

(Makes twelve mini pizzas)
One box English muffins
One jar pizza sauce
2 cups grated mozzarella cheese
Assorted pizza toppings (as desired)

1. Preheat oven to 350°.

2. Split English muffins in half.

3. Spread each muffin half with enough pizza sauce to cover (approximately 2 tablespoons).

4. Cover with grated mozzarella cheese and desired pizza toppings.

5. Bake for 10 to 15 minutes or until cheese melts and toppings are cooked.

Pirate's Grog

Ingredients

2 liter bottle ginger ale
2 liter bottle seltzer
1/2 gallon container orange juice
Orange sherbet (optional)

In punch bowl, combine seltzer, ginger ale, and orange juice. Chill well and stir slightly before serving. Optional: To create a frothy punch, add scoops of orange sherbet and mix slightly until foamy.

Child-sized Pirate Eye Patch

Materials

2-1/2" square piece of black poster board
1/4" black elastic
Pencil, scissors, tape measure, glue gun

1. Trace eye patch pattern onto poster board and cut out.

2. Wrap tape measure around child's head to determine amount of elastic needed. Subtract 1/2" to 1" and cut elastic so it is taut when on head.

3. Glue elastic ends to back of eye patch with glue gun.

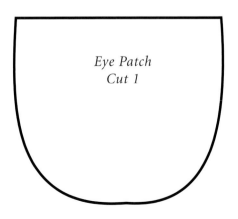

Eye Patch
Cut 1

Pirate Outfit
Designed by Barbara Czerniak

Thin red and white striped fabric is used to make the perfect pirate's outfit. The points on the tunic bottom add a roguish touch. Complete the outfit with a matching kerchief, belt, and eye patch. You and your bean bag friends will soon be saying things like "Arrrgh, matey" and "Ahoy, ye scurvy lads."

Tunic

Materials

6" x 24" piece of red and white striped fabric
2" x 24" piece of iron-on interfacing
Bias tape
Thread to match fabric
Pins, scissors, needle, pencil

1. Iron interfacing along bottom edge of fabric's wrong side. Interfacing will cover 2" of the fabric's 6" width. Make sure interfacing is securely bonded.

2. Fold fabric, placing right sides together to create a 6" x 12" rectangle. Place pattern for tunic front on the fold so that the distance from the bottom of the tunic points to the top of the interfacing measures approximately 1". Pin tunic back to fabric so that the distance from the tunic points to the top of the interfacing is also 1". Cut out.

3. Mark dot on tunic back with pencil.

4. On front and back pieces, sew top stitching along tunic points 1/8" from edge.

5. With right sides together, pin and stitch tunic backs with a 1/8" seam from lower back edge to dot (on pattern). Press seam open all the way to neck edge.

6. Starting at neck edge, stitch pressed seam allowance to notch, turn fabric, and continue up other side to create "V"-shaped opening.

7. With right sides together, sew back of tunic to front at shoulders with a 1/8" seam. Press seams to back.

8. Measure bias tape needed to finish neck opening by starting at back neck edge and going around entire neck opening. Add 1/2" and cut bias tape.

9. Fold under ends of bias tape 1/4" to wrong side and press.

10. Cover raw neck edge with bias tape, starting at one neck edge and continuing around to other edge. Baste in place with needle and thread.

11. Machine stitch bias tape in place.

12. Turn edges of each sleeve under 1/8". Stitch sleeve edge.

13. With right sides together, start at sleeve edge and sew sides together with a 1/8" seam, pivoting under arm and continuing to pointed bottom edge.

14. At each under arm, make one small cut through both pieces of fabric to the pivot point. **Do not cut stitching**.

15. Turn tunic right side out and press.

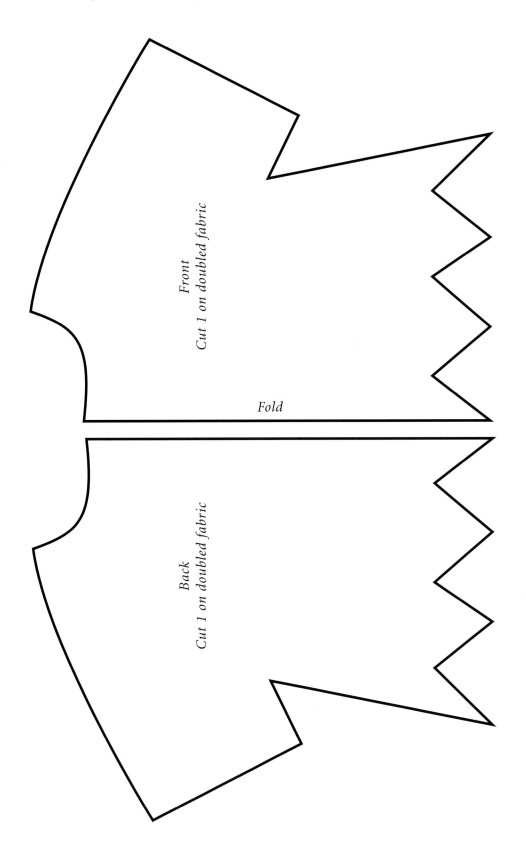

Front
Cut 1 on doubled fabric

Fold

Back
Cut 1 on doubled fabric

Eye Patch

Materials

Scrap piece of black felt
8-1/2" piece of 1/8" black elastic
Black thread
Pins, scissors

1. Place eye patch pattern onto scrap piece of felt.

2. Pin and cut out.

3. Measure elastic needed by wrapping elastic around toy's head until ends meet. Subtract 1/2" from this measurement and cut.

4. Stitch both ends of elastic to wrong side of eye patch by hand or machine.

Eye Patch
Cut 1

Kerchief

1. With right sides together, fold fabric to create a 5" x 7-1/2" rectangle.

2. Pin kerchief pattern to fabric, placing on fold line as indicated and cut out.

3. Press raw edge of kerchief to wrong side, about 1/4".

4. Stitch along folded edges. Press.

Materials

5" x 15" piece of red and white striped fabric
Thread to match fabric
Pins, scissors, iron

Belt

1. Measure the bean bag toy's waist.

2. Add 1/2" to this length and cut felt this length by 3/4" wide.

3. Wrap felt piece around toy and mark snap or Velcro placement.

4. With needle and thread, sew snap set or Velcro in place. Trim excess fabric if needed.

Materials

10" x 3/4" piece of black felt
Snap set or Velcro fastener
Black thread
Tape measure, scissors, needle

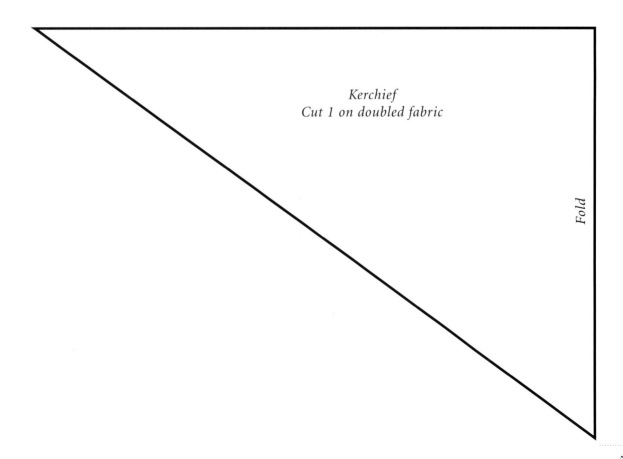

Kerchief
Cut 1 on doubled fabric

Fold

Pirate Galleon

You and your bean bag toys can sail the seven seas in search of treasure aboard this pirate galleon made from a half-gallon milk carton, poster board, and other materials readily found around the house. So grab your bean bag toys and set sail for adventure!

1. Cut two galleon patterns and one deck pattern from black poster board. (Note: Both pattern pieces need to be enlarged.)

2. Align back bottom edge of one galleon side cut-out with back edge of carton. Glue to sides of carton. Repeat for other side.

3. Glue wrong sides of bowsprit together to form curved ship front. Let dry.

4. Align back flat edge of ship deck piece with back edge of carton top. Glue in place. Angled front corners will fit into curve of ship's bow. Let dry.

5. To complete boat's stern, cut a 3-3/4" x 3-3/4" square from black poster board. Glue square onto back of carton.

6. To make portholes, trace outline of nickel onto aluminum foil ten times and cut out with scissors. Glue five portholes to each side of ship.

7. With a pencil, mark the ship masts' placement on deck piece. Using electric drill and 1/4" bit, drill holes into ship's deck at pencil marks.

8. To make ship's rear sails, cut two rectangles (5" x 7-1/4" and 4-1/2" x 6-1/4") from white paper or poster board. To make front sails, cut two additional rectangles (3-1/2" x 5-1/2" and 3-1/2"x 4-3/4"). Cut slits in top and bottom of sail pieces to insert mast.

9. To make pirate emblem for sail, cut a 2" x 2-1/2" rectangle from black poster board. Using a pencil, sketch skull, and crossbones onto peel-and-stick label. Outline sketch with black marker and cut out with scissors. Peel away backing and stick in center of black rectangle. Glue in center of 6-1/4" x 4-1/2" sail piece.

10. Cut dowel into 17-1/2" and 12-1/2" lengths. Insert dowel into slits on sails, placing larger rear and front sail pieces onto dowel first. (Larger sails are closest to the deck, smaller ones on top.)

11. Insert masts with sails into hole on deck. With glue gun, glue masts in place, if desired, and adjust sails as needed.

Materials

Black poster board
White poster board
 or paper
3-1/4" x 4" white
 peel-and-stick
 label
1/4" wooden dowel,
 30" long
1/2 gallon milk or
 juice carton
Nickel
Aluminum foil, razor
 blade or craft
 knife, glue*, glue
 gun, black marker,
 scissors, ruler,
 pencil, electric
 drill, 1/4" drill
 bit, hand saw

Used in this project:
Aleene's Tacky Glue

Project Note:
Hot glue does not
 adhere well to the
 milk carton's waxy
 sides. Use a thick
 white glue instead.
 The glue gun is
 used to secure the
 masts in place.

Caution!
Adult supervision is
 needed for this
 project.

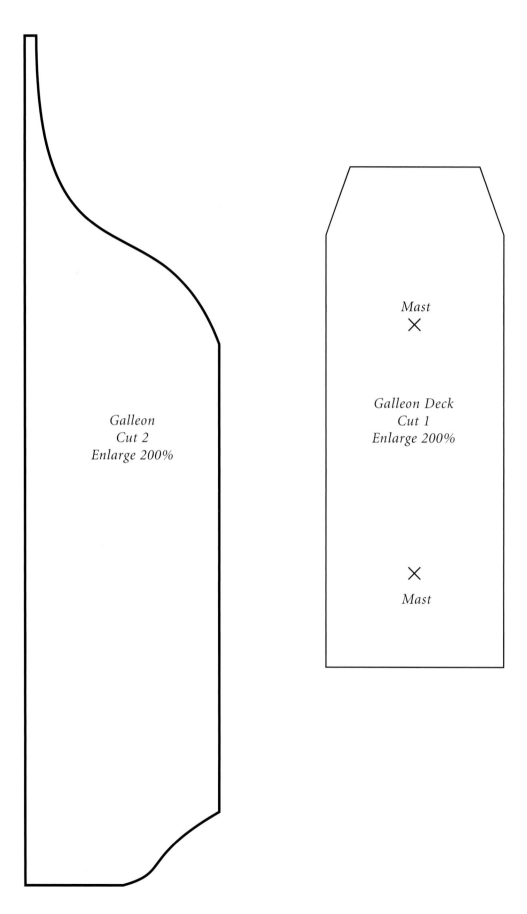

Galleon
Cut 2
Enlarge 200%

Mast
✕

Galleon Deck
Cut 1
Enlarge 200%

✕
Mast

Palm Trees

You can almost feel the sea breeze and hear the seagulls cry when you make these quick and easy palm trees. Paper towel, toilet tissue, or gift wrap tubes can be used for tree trunks. Palm fronds are made from green tissue paper gathered and then fringed with scissors.

1. Cut two 10" squares from green tissue paper. Cut tube into 8" length.

2. Place one sheet on top of the other and rotate to create diamond pattern shown (Fig. 1).

3. Create palm tree top by gathering tissue in center (Fig. 2).

4. Insert tree top into cardboard tube (Fig. 3).

5. To create palm fronds, cut slits in protruding tissue with scissors (Fig. 4).

6. Repeat Steps 2 through 5 to create additional trees with trunks of different lengths.

Materials

Green tissue paper
Paper towel, toilet tissue, or gift wrap tube
Scissors

Fig. 1

Fig. 2

Fig. 3

Fig. 4

Treasure Box

Pirates may have buried their treasure, but you'll want to show it off in this beautiful box! Multi-colored acrylic jewels are hot glued to a gold papier mâché box. Once the box is decorated, it's a great place to store your chocolate pieces of eight and other treasures.

Materials

4" x 4" x 2" papier
   mâché box
Gold spray paint
One bag acrylic
   jewels
Foil-covered choco-
   late coins, old
   jewelry, and other
   trinkets
Glue or glue gun

1. Spray-paint exterior and interior of box and lid with gold spray paint, following manufacturer's directions. Let dry.

2. Glue jewels to box sides and lid in desired pattern with bottled glue or glue gun.

3. Fill decorated box with chocolate coins, jewelry, and other trinkets.

Chapter 7

4th of July Barbecue

What would summertime be without a backyard barbecue? The 4th of July—America's birthday—is a great time for one. Some bean bag toys, like the Beanie Baby "Glory," are made from red, white, and blue patterned fabric and permanently show their patriotic colors. The bean bag toy shown in this chapter displays its spirit by wearing a patriotic print apron and complementary chef's hat. It's time to fire up the grill and cook traditional American favorites—hot dogs and hamburgers.

The picnic table and benches are made from wooden screen lath which can be purchased from a home center or lumber yard. The centerpiece is made from bandanna print fabric squares tucked into a 2" woven basket with the handle removed. American flags on toothpicks (purchased from a party store) are inserted among the fabric squares to complete the centerpiece.

After eating, grab your friends for a game of baseball or pack up your bean bag toy and head to a local park to watch a parade or fireworks.

Let's head for the backyard and fire up the grill. It's easy to tell who's in charge of cooking with this cute outfit—just look for the bean bag toy in the apron and chef's hat. No matter what the food tastes like, your toy will look great!

Decorations

Anything red, white, and blue makes a great decoration for a 4th of July celebration. Flags, crepe paper streamers, and balloons create a festive atmosphere. For a quick dessert that looks as good as it tastes, try the recipe for a red, white, and blue trifle. Or if you want a dessert that's easy to take with you to the park or fireworks display, bake cupcakes in flag motif cake cups and decorate them with red, white, and blue royal icing flags on top of your favorite flavor frosting.

Check your local party store for 4th of July decorations. These cake cups, flag toothpicks, and icing decorations all have a patriotic theme.

Activities

• Host your own 4th of July parade. Dress kids up in red, white, and blue clothing, decorate their bikes with crepe paper streamers, and have them parade up and down your block.

• Have a patriotic sing along. Let the children choose and sing songs like "Yankee Doodle," "The Star Spangled Banner," "My Country 'Tis of Thee," "You're a Grand Old Flag," and "America the Beautiful."

• Keep kids safe with explosive-free firecrackers: buy strips of air bubble packing material. When wadded up and wrung with the hands, the popping bubbles create sounds similar to exploding firecrackers.

Food
Red, White, and Blue Trifle

Ingredients

(Serves eight)
One angel food cake or pound cake
One package vanilla pudding
1 pint fresh raspberries or strawberries
1 pint fresh blueberries
Whipped cream

1. Wash and drain berries.

2. Break or cut cake into 1" cubes.

3. Make pudding according to package directions.

4. In a glass bowl, create a layer of cake cubes using half of cubed cake.

5. Cover cake cubes with approximately half of pudding mixture.

6. Sprinkle pudding layer with three-quarters of raspberries, making sure some berries are close to the edge of the bowl so they will show. (Remaining berries will be used to decorate top of trifle.)

7. Place the remaining cake cubes on top of raspberry layer.

8. Cover cake cubes with remaining pudding mixture.

9. Sprinkle pudding layer with three-quarters of blueberries, making sure to place berries close to the edge of the bowl so they will show. (Remaining berries will be used to decorate top of trifle.)

10. Cover layer of blueberries with whipped cream. Decorate with remaining berries.

Best-ever Burgers

Ingredients

(Makes four large burgers)
1 lb. hamburger
Half of medium onion, finely chopped
3 Tbs. ketchup
1 tsp. Worcestershire sauce

1. In a bowl, combine hamburger, onion, ketchup, and Worcestershire sauce, mixing ingredients with hands.

2. Form into patties.

3. Cook on stove top or grill until done.

Chef's Outfit

An apron and chef's hat will have your toy looking smart and keep it clean while cooking. Patriotic print fabric for the apron ties into the 4th of July theme.

Apron

Materials

*5" x 6" piece of
patriotic print
cotton or cotton
blend fabric
23" of 1/2" wide
white bias tape
White thread
Scissors, pins, iron*

1. Fold fabric with right sides together to make a 3" x 5" rectangle. Pin pattern to fabric, placing pattern fold line on fabric fold. Cut out.

2. Cut 3" piece of bias tape. Pin and sew tape in place across apron top, covering raw fabric edge. Trim ends.

3. Cut 5" piece of bias tape. Pin and sew tape in place across apron bottom, covering raw fabric edge. Trim ends.

4. Cut two 3" pieces of bias tape. On each piece, fold one end under 1/4" and press.

5. On each apron side, align folded bias tape end with bottom edge of apron. Pin in place and sew bias tape to apron sides, covering raw fabric edge. Bias tape edge should end at bottom of apron arm curve.

6. Cut a 23-1/2" piece of bias tape. Fold ends under 1/4" and press. At each end of bias tape, measure 6-1/2". Fold and pin bias tape from end to that point. On each side, beginning at the 6-1/2" mark, pin bias tape to apron arm curve, covering remaining raw fabric edge and ending at apron top. Fold section of bias tape extending from apron top around neck in half and pin to make apron neck opening. Repeat process on other side.

7. Starting at one apron tie, stitch from one end of the tape to the other, stitching through fabric of apron arm curves and ending at opposite apron tie.

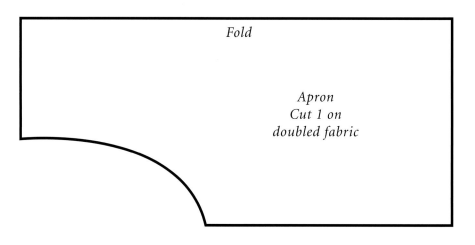

Fold

*Apron
Cut 1 on
doubled fabric*

Chef's Hat

1. To make hat base, cut piece of paper roll 1-1/4" long.

2. Measure circumference of roll and add 1/4". Cut piece of paper this length by 1-1/4" wide.

3. Glue paper onto towel roll. Trim edges if needed.

4. Turn paper seam to back. To make ear holes, draw a 1" wide x 3/4" high arc on each side of the hat base using a compass and cut out.

5. Trace 8" circle onto fabric and cut it out.

6. With needle and thread, sew running stitch 1/4" from fabric edge. Pull thread to gather fabric, making the opening of the gathers the same size as the circumference of the towel roll. Secure thread.

7. Using glue gun, glue gathered fabric to inside of hat base.

Materials

*Paper towel or toilet
    paper roll
White paper
9" square piece of
    white cotton fabric
White thread
Glue, scissors,
    compass, needle,
    glue gun, pencil*

Picnic Table and Benches

After a long day of playing outside, your bean bag toys can take a well-deserved rest and enjoy a picnic on this pint-sized wooden table with matching benches. A backyard picnic is a great way to welcome the newest member of your collection and introduce him or her to your other bean bag toys. Why not invite friends and their toys to join the celebration? With this project, the toys can have a table of their own to get to know each other better.

Picnic Table

1. To make table legs, cut two 4" pieces of screen lath. Sand ends if needed. Glue together with glue gun to form an "X" shape. Repeat this step to create a second set of legs. Set aside.

2. To make table top, cut five 10" lengths of screen lath. Sand ends if needed and place pieces face down, side by side, 1/8" apart.

3. To make leg braces, cut six 4" lengths of screen lath. Cut two of these pieces in half lengthwise to create four 3/8" wide lengths.

4. On the back of the table top, glue a 3/8" x 4" lath strip from Step 3 perpendicularly, 1/2" from each edge of the table top. Let dry.

5. Take table legs and saw ends of both leg sets to fit flush with table top and to sit level on ground.

6. Glue legs to inside of 3/8" strip. Glue a second 3/8" strip to inside of each table leg to create a brace for table legs. Let dry.

Materials

7 ft. wooden screen lath
Saw, glue gun, sandpaper

Benches

1. Cut four 10", four 1-1/4", and four 2" pieces of screen lath. Sand ends if needed.

2. To make picnic bench, place two 10" lengths face down, 1/8" apart. Glue 1-1/4" lath piece perpendicularly, 1/2" from each bench end.

3. To make bench legs, take two 2" pieces of screen lath and place on top of each other. Glue together with glue gun to form an "X" shape. Repeat to create a second set of legs.

4. Saw ends of both leg sets to fit flush with table top and to sit level on ground.

5. Glue legs to outside of 1-1/4" piece.

6. Repeat Steps 1 though 5 to make second picnic bench.

Materials

7 ft. wooden screen lath
Saw, glue gun, sandpaper

Materials

2-1/2" woven basket
Modeling clay
Three American flag toothpicks
Three 2" x 2" red bandanna print fabric squares
Three 2" x 2" blue bandanna print fabric squares
Scissors, glue (optional)

Fig. 1

Fig. 2

Fig. 3

Fig. 4

Flag Centerpiece

You don't have to be a Betsy Ross to make this centerpiece. If you can cut and fold fabric you can make this quick and easy no-sew project! Red and blue bandanna print fabric was used here, but any red and blue fabric will work.

1. Remove basket handle with scissors.

2. Place flags into modeling clay (Fig. 1).

3. Place clay in bottom of basket. Secure in place by gluing or pressing clay into basket (Fig. 2).

4. Bunch bandanna fabric squares at center so wrong side of fabric is inside folded square (Fig. 3).

5. Place folded squares into basket, alternating red and blue fabric around modeling clay base (Fig. 4). Adjust squares and flags as needed.

Chapter 8

Beach Party

If you wish summer could last all year long, grab your sunscreen and shades and let's head for the beach! No matter what month of the year it is, you can always head to the shore in your imagination. Our bean bag toys are soaking up the sun in anchor-print swim trunks and a coordinating one-piece swimsuit with a skirt cover-up.

For fun in the sun, let your bean bag toys make sand castles with a miniature sand bucket made from a painted plastic condiment container with a chenille stem handle. Protecting delicate skin from the sun's rays, a sun bonnet made from a store-bought straw hat decorated with a silk flower and grosgrain ribbon sits jauntily on the head of our bovine bathing beauty. Toys can lie leisurely on a beach towel cut from a hand towel or wash cloth; hem fabric edges to keep terry cloth from fraying. Stenciled party invitations and suggested activities continue the beach theme.

This store-bought chair is perfect for your bean bag toy to relax in at the beach. But don't forget accessories for fun in the sun like a towel, sun hat, and bucket.

There's no place like the beach to relax and get away from it all—even for bean bag toys! But what if you live a thousand miles from the coast? No problem. If you've got a sandbox in your backyard, you can make your own beach. (See Chapter 6 for palm tree instructions)

Activities

• Don't know what to do with the shells you collected from the beach while on vacation? Use them to decorate a picture frame and insert a photo from your vacation into it.

• Make sand cast candles. In a bucket, mix sand with water until sand is moist and scoopable. Form a shape several inches deep by scooping out sand using your hands or kitchen utensils. Tie a wick to a pencil or dowel and position over the center of the sand shape, making sure the wick extends down to the bottom of the shape in the sand. Melt paraffin wax, pour into the shape and fill. Allow wax to harden. Remove candle from sand and trim wick with scissors. Note: Adult supervision is needed for this project.

• When rubbed into sand, colored chalk makes beautiful colored sand. Create lovely decorative accents by layering sand inside glass containers. To make interesting patterns, place a toothpick next to the edge of the container and poke it through the sand layers. Leftover colored sand can even be used to decorate various objects. Drizzle glue on cards, picture frames, bottles, or other items and pour sand over the glue and let dry. Brush off excess.

Swim Trunks

Surf's up! Your bean bag toy will look mighty cute in his swim trunks as he catches some rays. The adjustable drawstring waistband keeps his trunks secure and comfortable should he decide to do some bodysurfing. Whether in the surf or on the shore, he's sure to be the envy of every other guy on the beach.

Materials

*6" x 9" piece of
    cotton or cotton
    blend anchor print
    fabric*
*12" of 1/8" wide
    satin ribbon*
*Thread to match
    fabric*
Pins, small safety pin

1. Fold fabric to create a 3" x 9" rectangle. Pin pattern to fabric, placing pattern fold line along fabric fold. Cut out. Repeat so you have two trunks pieces.

2. To hem leg openings, fold under bottom edge of both trunks pieces 1/8" and stitch.

3. With right sides together, sew a 1/8" seam along diagonal of one piece to form leg opening. Repeat for second piece.

4. Open sewn trunks sections. Beginning at waist of trunks, with right sides together, pin sections together. Sew continuous seam from front through trunks crotch to back.

5. Fold and sew 1/4" casing at waist, leaving small opening at trunks front.

6. Pin small safety pin to satin ribbon. Thread through casing.

7. Place trunks on toy and adjust waist gathering by pulling on the ribbon ends. Tie ribbon in a bow.

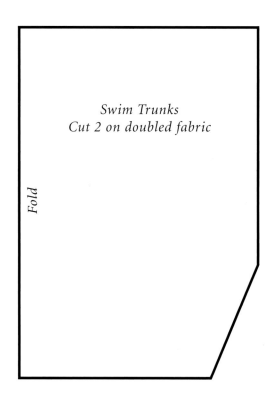

*Swim Trunks
Cut 2 on doubled fabric*

Fold

Swimsuit and Skirt Cover-up

Designed by Barbara Czerniak

This bovine bathing beauty looks "udderly" delightful in her one-piece stretch swimsuit with coordinating skirt cover-up. After a day of soaking up the sun—using sunscreen, of course—she can put on the skirt cover-up and head into town for a milk shake and a grilled cheese sandwich.

Swimsuit

Materials

6" x 12" piece of stretchable lightweight fleece (fabric should stretch along 12" length)

6" piece of rope elastic

15" of 1/8" satin ribbon to match fabric

Thread to match fabric

Needle, large-eyed needle, small safety pin, scissors, pins

1. Pin swimsuit front pattern to fabric so single thickness of fabric stretches from side to side. Cut out.

2. With right sides together, fold remaining fabric in half, again making sure fabric stretches from side to side.

3. Pin swimsuit back pattern to fabric, placing pattern on fold as indicated. Cut out.

4. Turn fabric on top back section to wrong side 1/4" and stitch along fabric edge.

5. Stitch one end of elastic to casing opening. Do not stitch casing closed.

6. Using small safety pin or large-eyed needle, thread 6" piece of rope elastic through casing and gather fabric to 3" length.

7. Stitch elastic to fabric to secure. Trim excess elastic if necessary.

8. With right sides together, place swimsuit back on swimsuit front. First, pin sides together, then pin crotch sections together. Sew sides and crotch sections with 1/8" seams.

9. Finish upper front sides of swimsuit by turning fabric under 1/8" to wrong side. Pin in place and stitch with needle and thread.

10. Turn swimsuit top front under 1/4" to wrong side. Sew close to fabric's edge.

11. Thread ribbon through casing using large-eyed needle.

12. Secure ribbon at casing opening by stitching through fabric and ribbon with needle and thread.

13. Finish leg openings with 1/8" hem. Sew with needle and thread.

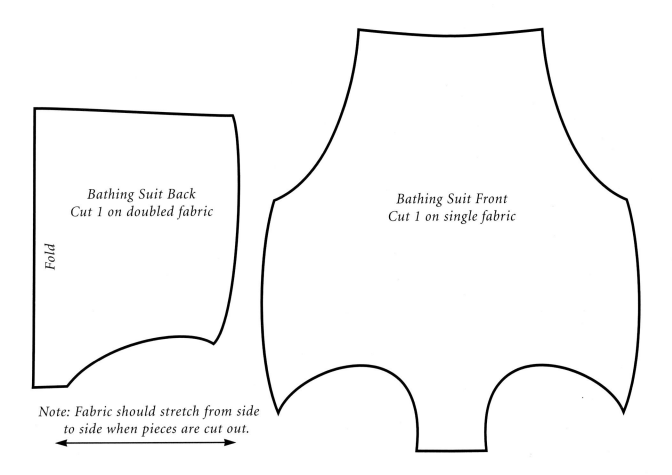

*Bathing Suit Back
Cut 1 on doubled fabric*

Fold

*Bathing Suit Front
Cut 1 on single fabric*

*Note: Fabric should stretch from side
to side when pieces are cut out.*

Skirt Cover-up

1. With right sides together, fold fabric in half lengthwise to make a 4" x 7-1/2" rectangle.

2. To make skirt back center seam, pin and sew raw edges of 4" side together with 1/8" seam. Press seam to one side.

3. Sew 1/2" casing along top edge of skirt, leaving a small opening near back center seam.

4. Cut a 6" piece of 1/8" elastic. Attach small safety pin to one end of elastic and thread through casing.

5. Make sure opposite end of elastic does not go through casing. Sew elastic ends together.

6. Sew 1/4" hem along skirt bottom. Press skirt when completed.

Materials

*4" x 15" piece of
  anchor print poly-
  cotton blend fabric
6" of 1/8" elastic
Thread to match
  fabric
Pins, small safety
  pin, iron*

Seashell Invitations

Stenciled invitations with a seashore motif are easy to make. Simply choose your favorite colors of paint and, using a pre-cut stencil, dab the paint on the note cards with a stencil brush as shown.

1. Squeeze puddles of paint onto plastic plate (Fig. 1).

2. Lay card on flat surface, front side up. Tape stencil onto card with masking tape.

3. Dip brush in desired paint color and blot excess paint on plate surface.

4. Dab paint onto stencil openings, moving from edge to center of cut-out. Finish all same-colored cut-outs before changing paint color (Fig. 2).

5. Rinse brush thoroughly with water. Proceed with additional colors until card is completed.

6. Carefully remove stencil. Set card aside to dry.

7. Clean stencil thoroughly before using on next card.

Fig. 1

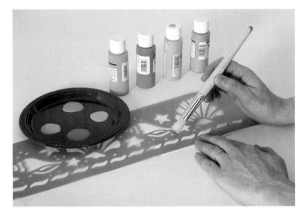

Fig. 2

Materials

Plastic plate
Stencil brush
Pink, green, and gold acrylic paint*
Shell stencil**
Blank greeting cards with envelopes***
Masking tape

Used in this project:
*Ceramcoat Pretty Pink and Ocean Reef acrylic paints
*Plaid FolkArt Harvest Gold acrylic paint
**Plaid Stencil #28911 "Seashells by the Seashore"
***Strathmore Blank Greeting Cards #105-12 "Palm Beach White"

Watch your bean bag toy cheer on your favorite team in this cheerleader's outfit made from felt and flannel. We used red, white, and blue here, but you can substitute your school's colors for the outfit and pompoms. Go team!

Chapter 9

After The Game

Football, baseball, soccer, basketball, swimming, volleyball. You name it—everyone loves sports. If you kick it, bounce it, dribble it, or hit it, we'll cheer for it. Show your support by dressing your bean bag toy in your team's colors and cheer your players on at the game. If your team's mascot is an animal, find a bean bag toy that represents it and take it to the game as a good luck charm. Afterwards, celebrate your win or commiserate your loss at a party with players and friends.

Decorations

• Poster board and paint make great signs to take to the game. Pick team colors for accents and make letters large enough to read from a distance.
• Celebrate the win with a shower of confetti made from small squares of construction paper.
• Make a team pennant from poster board cut into a triangle and a dowel. Draw your team's mascot with markers and color with acrylic paint. Glue poster board triangle to dowel.
• Make banners by painting slogans in acrylic paint on old sheets.

Food
Celebration Sundae

1. Scoop your favorite flavor ice cream into a bowl.

2. Sprinkle candy pieces on top of ice cream.

3. Pour hot fudge sauce over ice cream.

4. Squirt whipped cream on top of candy pieces.

5. Sprinkle whipped cream with chopped nuts, if desired.

6. Top with a maraschino cherry.

Ingredients

*Assorted flavors of
 ice cream
Chopped candy
 pieces and crushed
 candy bars
Hot fudge sauce
 (recipe follows)
Canned whipped
 cream
Chopped nuts
Maraschino cherries*

Hot Fudge Sauce

Ingredients

*(Makes approx-
    imately 2 cups)*
*1-1/2 cup
    granulated sugar*
1/2 cup brown sugar
3/4 cup cocoa
1/4 cup flour
1/4 tsp. salt
*14 oz. can evapo-
    rated milk*
*1 Tbs. butter (do not
    use margarine)*
1 cup water
2 tsp. vanilla

1. In a sauce pan, combine sugars, cocoa, flour, and salt. Add milk, butter, and water.

2. Bring to a boil over medium heat. Cook five minutes.

3. Remove from heat and let cool.

4. Stir in vanilla.

Seven Layer Dip

Ingredients

*One can refried
    beans*
*One container frozen
    guacamole*
*One medium onion,
    chopped*
One tomato, chopped
*1 cup grated cheddar
    cheese*
1 pint sour cream
*One small can
    chopped black
    olives*
Tortilla chips

1. Allow guacamole to thaw.

2. Spread refried beans in a small casserole dish.

3. Spread guacamole on top of refried beans.

4. Top guacamole with a layer of chopped onions.

5. Place chopped tomato on top of onions.

6. Sprinkle cheddar cheese on top of tomatoes.

7. Spread sour cream on top of cheddar cheese.

8. Sprinkle chopped olives on top of sour cream.

9. Serve with tortilla chips.

Cheerleader Outfit

Our bean bag toy is dressed and ready to cheer in a pleated felt skirt and coordinating top. Pompoms in two sizes are easy to make from yarn. So, rev up your spirit and go team!

Top

1. Fold felt in half to create a rectangle shape. Pin shirt patterns to felt, making sure to place pattern fold line on fabric fold. Cut out.

2. With right sides together, pin shirt back pieces to front at sides and shoulder.

3. Sew 1/8" seam at sides and shoulders.

Materials

One 9" x 12" white felt square
Two snap sets
12" blue rickrack
Thread to match fabric
Pins, scissors, needle

4. Beginning at back neck edge on one side, pin rickrack around neck. Cut off excess. Sew in place.

5. Place shirt on bean bag toy and mark placement of the snap sets. Sew in place with needle and thread.

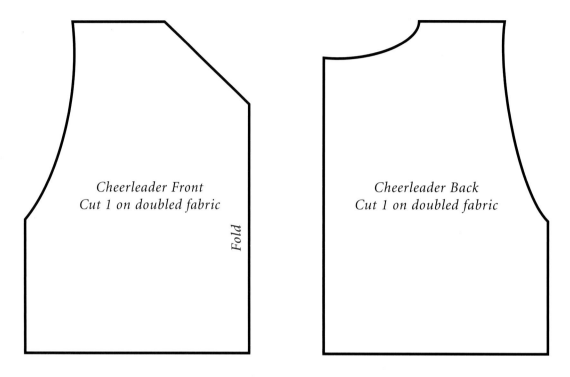

Cheerleader Front
Cut 1 on doubled fabric

Fold

Cheerleader Back
Cut 1 on doubled fabric

Skirt

Materials

2-3/4" x 18" piece of red flannel
10" red bias tape
Snap set
Thread to match fabric
Pins, scissors, tape measure, needle, iron, pencil, ruler, tape

1. Tape pattern pieces together.

2. Pin pattern to fabric, marking pleats as shown with pencil and ruler. Cut out.

3. Turn skirt bottom under 1/8" and sew.

4. Pin pleats and stitch each pleat with 1/2" seam.

5. Measure waistline. Add 1/2" and cut bias tape to this measurement.

6. Fold ends of bias tape under 1/4" and press.

7. Fold and pin bias tape over waist and stitch in place.

8. Wrap skirt around bean bag toy's waist and mark snap placement. Sew with needle and thread.

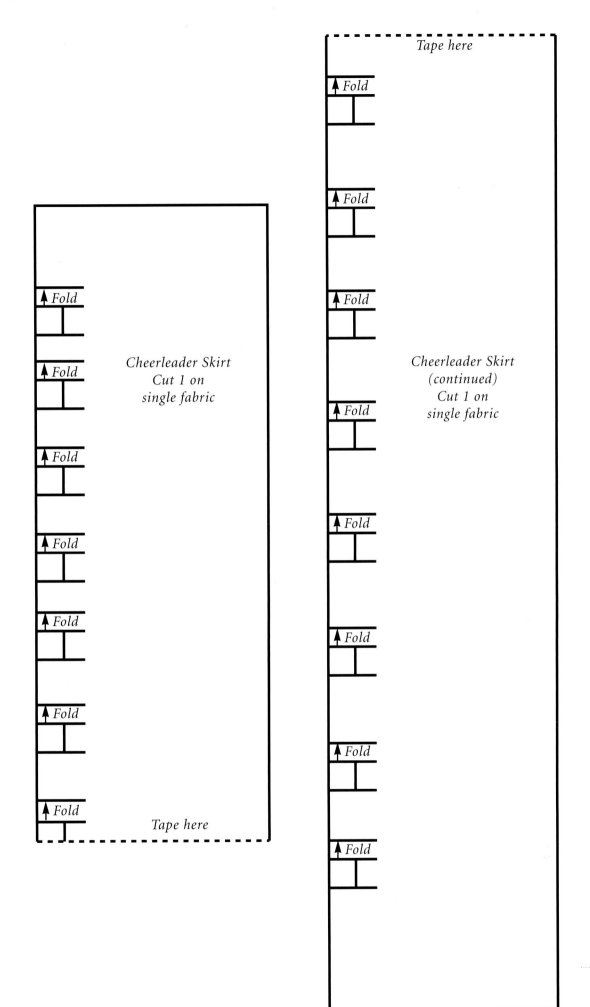

Tape here

↑ *Fold*

↑ *Fold*

↑ *Fold*

*Cheerleader Skirt
Cut 1 on
single fabric*

↑ *Fold*

↑ *Fold*

↑ *Fold*

↑ *Fold*

↑ *Fold*

Tape here

↑ *Fold*

↑ *Fold*

↑ *Fold*

↑ *Fold*

*Cheerleader Skirt
(continued)
Cut 1 on
single fabric*

↑ *Fold*

↑ *Fold*

↑ *Fold*

↑ *Fold*

Pompoms

Materials

3" x 5" piece of thick cardboard
Red, white, and blue yarn
Scissors

Fig. 1

Fig. 2

Fig. 3

Fig. 4

Fig. 5

1. Wrap white yarn around narrow width of cardboard thirty times (Fig. 1). Cut yarn.

2. On top of white yarn, wrap blue yarn around the cardboard thirty times. Cut yarn.

3. On top of blue yarn, wrap red yarn around the cardboard thirty times. Cut yarn.

4. Cut two 8" pieces of red yarn. Fold one piece in half to make a 4" doubled piece. Slide yarn piece along center of cardboard underneath wrapped yarn (Fig. 2).

5. Tie with a knot to gather yarn together.

6. Repeat Steps 4 and 5 on other side of cardboard.

7. Cut white, red, and blue yarn loops at top and bottom of cardboard, making two pompoms (Fig. 3).

8. Hold pompom by red yarn ties and fluff yarn (Figs. 4 and 5).

9. Finished pompoms can be tied onto bean bag toy's arms.

Note: If you want to make matching pompoms for your child, simply follow the above directions using an 8-1/2" x 11" piece of cardboard and increasing the number of times to wrap yarn around the cardboard from thirty to sixty.

Chapter 10

Halloween Party

Trick or Treat! Little ghosts and goblins will love dressing up their bean bag toys in darling costumes and going door to door with them. The witch sports a cape and broom which can be made at home. Her hat and the picket fence she's perched on were purchased at a craft store. Who can resist the candy corn costume? It makes your toy look almost good enough to eat! When the pumpkin costume is gathered, it adjusts easily to your toy's size.

Decorations

• Dry ice always lends an eerie atmosphere. Check to see if you can special order it from a grocery store or dairy.

• Check party stores for tapes of creepy sounds. Play them as children come to your door.

• Synthetic spider webbing can be stretched to cover large areas. It's great to stretch across tree limbs for a spooky effect.

• Make creepy bats from helium-filled black balloons with construction paper wings. Weight strings with pennies to keep them from flying away. Use peel-and-stick labels to make eyes and fangs.

• Ghoulish hands are great party favors. Candy corn placed in the tips of plastic food handling gloves look like fingernails. Fill the gloves with popcorn or snack mix and secure with wire twists or ribbons.

Who says Trick or Treating is for people only? Dressed as a witch, piece of candy corn, and pumpkin, these bean bag toys are ready to go door to door, too!

Witch Costume

Our cute little witch, shown on opposite page at top, is ready to fly off for a night of trick or treating. No eyes of newt or bat wings are needed for her to cast a spell over you. She's totally bewitching dressed in her cape and store-bought hat. Her broom is great for flying and for sweeping up Halloween candy wrappers around the house!

Cape

1. Sew 1/4" hem on sides and bottom of fabric.

2. To create ruffled collar on cape, fold top of fabric over 1" to wrong side and pin in place. Sew two lines of basting stitches, one 1/8" above raw edge of fabric and the other 1/4" above raw edge of fabric.

3. Gather fabric to 6" length. Secure threads with knots.

4. Sew snaps onto collar corners with needle and thread.

Materials

*8" x 16" piece of
    black cotton fabric*
Snap set
Black thread
Pins, scissors, needle

Broom

1. Wrap five or six raffia strands around the cardboard (Fig. 1).

2. Cut both ends of raffia to create small raffia pieces (Fig. 2).

3. Dab glue from glue gun onto dowel, approximately 1" from bottom (Fig. 3).

4. Grasp raffia broom straws with fingers (Fig. 4).

5. Stick dowel into center of broom straws, encircling dowel and placing edges of broom straws in glue. Raffia will extend approximately 2" past the bottom of the dowel (Fig. 5).

6. Select a long strand of raffia. Leaving a 3" piece loose, wrap remaining raffia around the top part of the broom straws ten times (Fig. 6).

7. Tie loose raffia ends into a square knot, securing broom straws to dowel (Fig. 7).

8. Trim excess raffia (Fig. 8).

Materials

Brown raffia
3-1/2" piece of
*   cardboard*
3/16" dowel, 6-1/2"
*   long*
Scissors, glue gun

Fig. 1

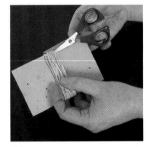

Fig. 2

Fig. 3

Fig. 4

Fig. 5

Fig. 6

Fig. 7

Fig. 8

Candy Corn Costume

Looking for a cute and clever gift to take to a Halloween party? This delicious little candy corn costume along with a bag of Halloween goodies is sure to please. To make the two-tone outfit, white and orange cotton blend fabric are sewn together and then the outfit is cut out.

1. Sew white and orange fabric pieces together along 16" side of fabric. Press seam toward white fabric.

2. Fold sewn fabric piece in half with right sides together, matching seams.

3. Pin pattern to fabric, matching line on pattern with seam. Cut out.

4. On costume front, mark and cut out circle head opening. Fold bias tape over raw edge of head opening and stitch in place.

5. To make arm opening, cut two 1" x 2-1/4" rectangles from remaining orange fabric. On costume front, with right sides together, place and pin rectangles as shown on pattern.

6. To create arm holes, stitch a 1/8" x 1-1/2" rectangle in the center of each fabric rectangle. Cut open center of stitching and make diagonal cuts to the corners of the rectangles. **Do not cut stitching**.

7. Pull fabric rectangle through opening to wrong side and press. Topstitch with orange thread around arm hole openings.

8. With right sides together, pin costume front to back. Beginning and ending 1" from bottom edge, stitch front of costume to back with a 1/8" seam, leaving a 4" opening across the bottom of the costume.

9. Turn under raw edges of bottom opening and topstitch with orange thread to finish.

Materials

7" x 16" piece of orange cotton fabric
3" x 16" piece of white cotton fabric
8" white bias tape
Needle
Orange and white thread
Pins, scissors, iron

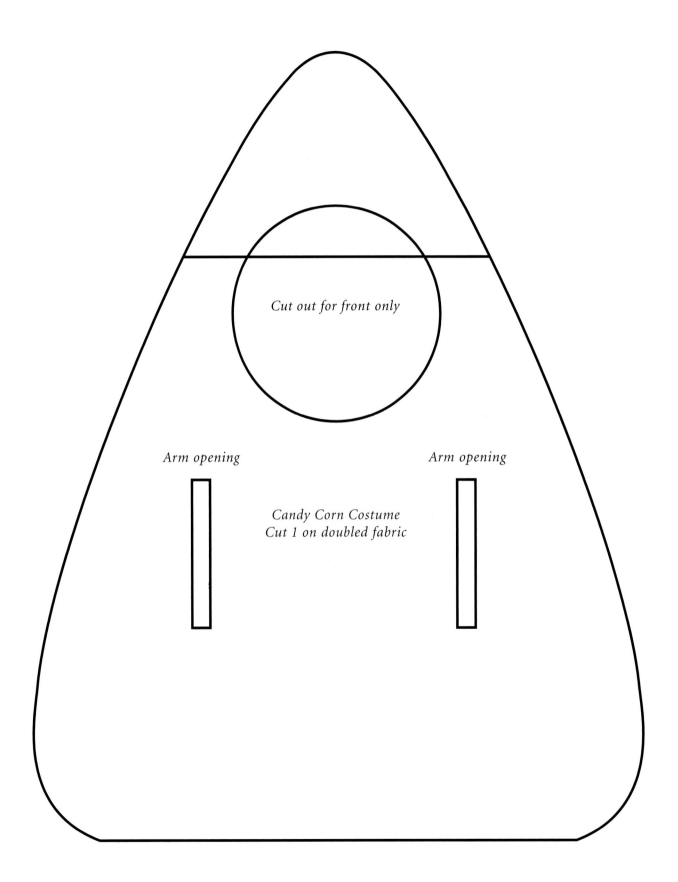

Cut out for front only

Arm opening   Arm opening

Candy Corn Costume
Cut 1 on doubled fabric

Pumpkin Costume

No time to go to the pumpkin patch? Don't worry. In this adorable costume, any toy can be transformed into your Halloween jack 'o lantern.

Materials

5" x 18" piece of orange cotton or cotton blend fabric
1 yard of 1/8" orange satin ribbon
1/2 yard of 1/4" green satin ribbon
Green and black felt
Orange and black (optional) thread
Pins, scissors, small safety pin, ruler or tape measure, needle (optional)

1. To make costume front, cut a 5" x 8-1/2" piece of orange fabric. Make costume back by cutting two 4-1/4" x 5" pieces of fabric.

2. With right sides together, pin back pieces to front.

3. On one side, sew a 1" side seam from top of costume. Leave 1-1/2" opening for arm hole. Resume sewing below opening and continue to bottom of costume. Repeat on other side.

4. Turn under raw edges of arm holes and topstitch with orange thread.

5. Sew 1/4" casing along top and bottom of costume.

6. With right sides together, pin and sew back center seam, leaving casing opening unsewn.

7. Cut orange ribbon in half, making two 18" lengths. Attach small safety pin to one ribbon's end and thread pin and ribbon through top casing. Repeat for bottom casing.

8. To make leaf necklace, cut 1/2" triangles from green felt.

9. Beginning and ending 4" from ends of green ribbon, pin triangles onto ribbon and sew in place.

10. Fold black felt in half. Pin eye and mouth patterns on felt, placing the mouth piece on the fold line, and cut out. Using needle and black thread, stitch onto front of costume, placing top of eyes 3/4" from top edge.

11. Put costume on toy. Grasp ribbon ends and create gathers by sliding fabric. Tie in place.

12. Tie leaf necklace around toy's neck or, if desired, tack by hand to costume top with needle and thread.

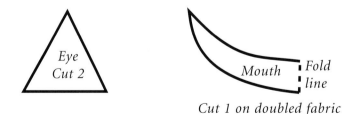

Eye Cut 2

Mouth | *Fold line*

Cut 1 on doubled fabric

Chapter 11

Slumber Party

Have you ever wondered why it's called a slumber party when the object seems to be to stay awake for as long as possible? There's no denying that slumber parties and sleep-overs are incredibly popular gatherings. Bean bag toys love slumber parties, too. Dress them in a comfy nightgown or wrap them in a robe and tuck them into a fleecy, warm sleeping bag. Just remember, too many ghost stories will keep your toys up, too!

Snacks and games are an important part of the party. Popcorn is a traditional favorite snack, but any finger food is sure to be snapped up. Try mini pizzas, egg rolls, or quiche instead of fatty chips and dip. A veggie platter with low-fat dressing is a great way to get kids to eat their vegetables.

Games

Flashlight Tag (Outside)

A flashlight and eight to ten people are needed to play. It must be dark.

Select a home base site and one person to be "it." This person takes the flashlight, hides his or her eyes, and counts to fifty. While the player who is "it" is counting, other players hide. Once the person with the flashlight counts to fifty, he or she turns on the flashlight and begins searching for other players. The goal is to get back to home base without being tagged by the flashlight beam. The first person to be tagged by the beam becomes the next person to be "it" and the game starts over.

Sardines (Inside)

Six to ten players are needed to play. All players, except one, need "mini" flashlights.

Determine guidelines about rooms where players can hide. Remove breakables from these rooms and turn out all lights in the rooms. Players all begin at one location which is home base. While one player hides, the other players hide their eyes and count to fifty. The remaining players split up and search for the hiding player with "mini" flashlights. If a player finds the person who's hiding he or she must turn out the light and join the hiding player. The name of the game comes from the fact that players eventually get caught because they are crammed into a hiding space like sardines in a can.

Slumber parties are lots of fun. With a robe, nightgown, and sleeping bag ensemble, your bean bag toys can join you and your friends as you stay up late and have fun.

Nightgown

Your bean bag toy will have sweet dreams in this comfy nightgown, shown on opposite page at left. The cotton blend, cloud patterned fabric used for this project is great for warm, summer nights. Consider using flannel for a nightgown that's sure to keep your toys warm on chilly fall and winter nights.

1. Fold fabric to create 7" x 13" rectangle. Pin patterns to fabric, placing pattern fold lines on fabric fold. Cut out.

2. On front of nightgown, sew two rows of basting stitches between notches along neckline edge. Gather fabric by pulling basting threads. Gathers should be 2-1/2" in length.

3. To make back neck opening, cut a 1-1/2" x 3/4" fabric facing from remaining fabric. With right sides together, pin facing to center neck edge of nightgown back. Stitch down facing 1-1/4", stitch across 1/8", and stitch back to neck edge 1-1/4". Cut down center of facing. Turn facing to inside and press. Turn neck edge under 1/8" and press. Topstitch along neck opening and facing.

4. Placing right sides together, start at neck gathering and pin front and back nightgown pieces together. Stitch from neck opening to top sleeve edge with a 1/8" seam. Then sew from bottom of sleeve edge along sleeve and down side to bottom of nightgown. Repeat on opposite side.

5. Turn sleeve edges under 1/8" and topstitch.

6. Fold 1/4" hem along bottom edge and sew. Turn nightgown right side out.

7. Measure sleeve openings and cut lace pieces to fit. Stitch to sleeve openings with needle and thread.

8. Measure neck opening and cut lace piece to fit. Stitch to neck opening with needle and thread.

Materials

7" x 26" piece of cloud print cotton or cotton blend fabric
16" piece of 1/2" wide lace
Thread to match fabric
Pins, scissors, needle, iron

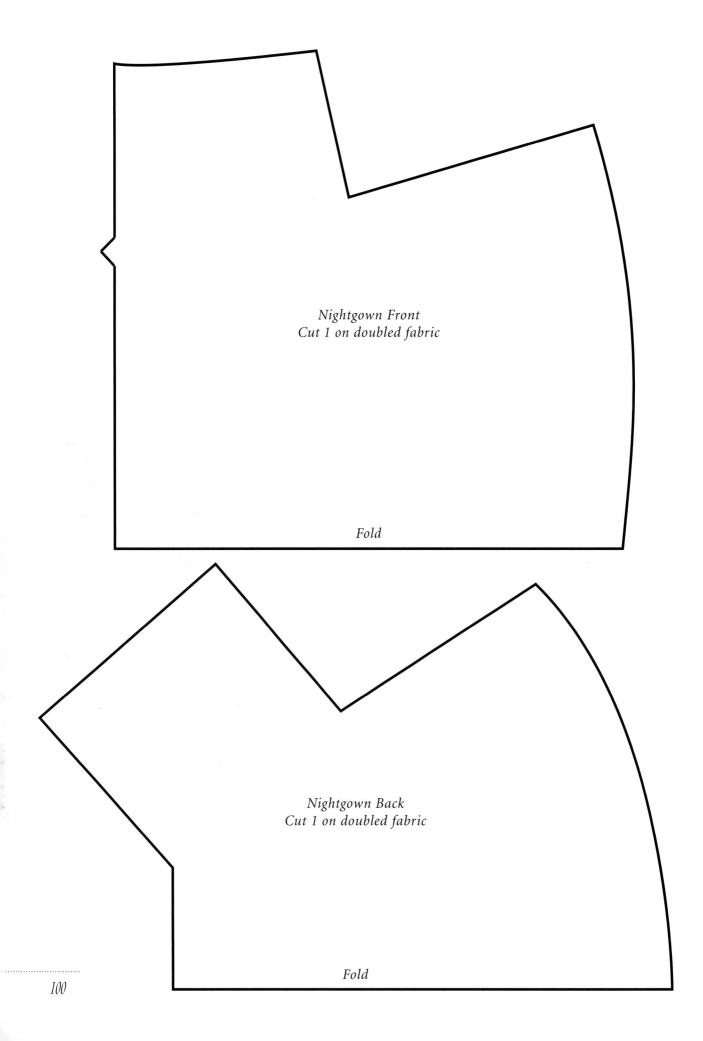

Nightgown Front
Cut 1 on doubled fabric

Fold

Nightgown Back
Cut 1 on doubled fabric

Fold

Robe

Whether sneaking down to the kitchen for a midnight snack or lounging around and watching TV, your bean bag toy is sure to be comfortable in this robe. The snowflake patterned fabric used coordinates nicely with the nightgown and sleeping bag (see pages 99 and 103, respectively). Try making the entire ensemble!

1. Fold fabric to create a 7" x 12" rectangle. Pin robe back to fabric, placing pattern fold on fabric fold. Cut out. On remaining fabric, pin left and right front pieces on single thickness of fabric and cut out.

2. With right sides together, pin left and right robe fronts to robe back.

3. On one side, stitch a 1/8" seam from neck opening to top sleeve edge. Then sew from bottom of sleeve edge along sleeve and down side to bottom of robe. Repeat on other side.

4. Turn sleeve edges under 1/8" and topstitch.

5. Beginning at square hem edge of robe front, place and pin raw fabric in center of bias tape, covering raw fabric edge. Continue along hem, up curved robe front, around neck edge and back down to starting point. Add 1/4", turning tape under to create finished edge.

6. Stitch bias tape, making sure to catch fabric edge in bias tape.

7. To make belt loop, cut two 1" lengths of bias tape. Turn cut edges under 1/8" and stitch to robe back, approximately 2" apart.

8. To make belt, cut 30" piece of bias tape. Fold tape in half. Turn under cut edges and pin. Stitch along all edges.

Materials

7" x 24" piece of snowflake print cotton or cotton blend fabric
1/2" bias tape to match fabric
Thread to match fabric and bias tape
Pins, scissors

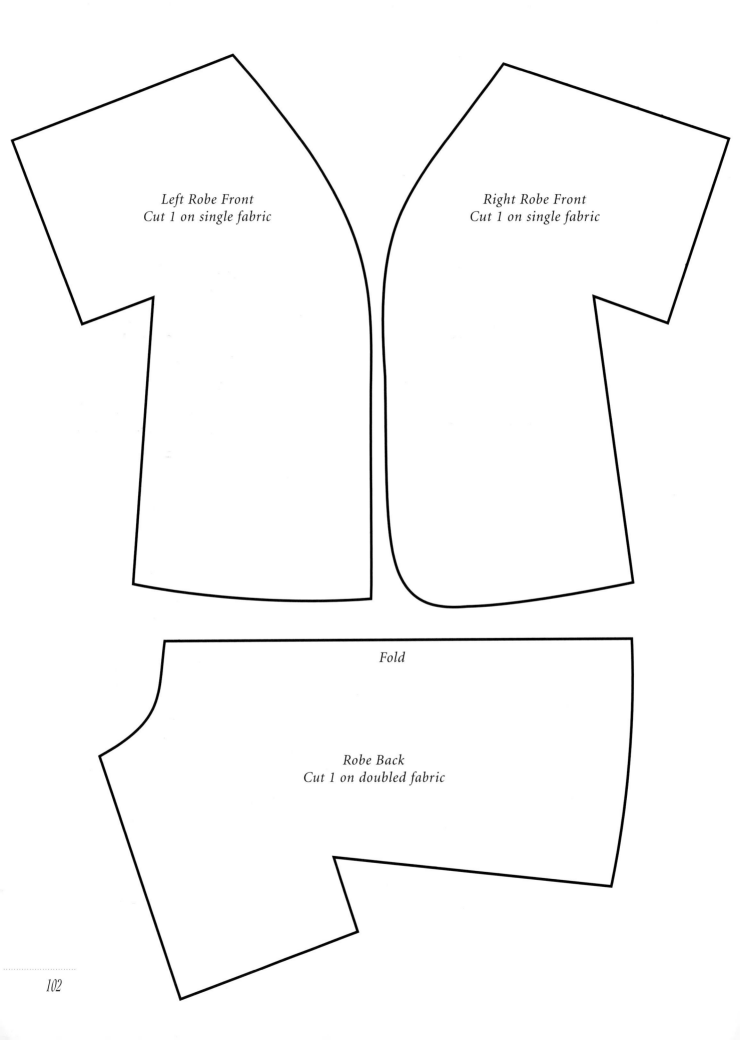

Left Robe Front
Cut 1 on single fabric

Right Robe Front
Cut 1 on single fabric

Fold

Robe Back
Cut 1 on doubled fabric

Sleeping Bag

Your bean bag friend will find it hard to stay awake when curling up in this soft, cozy sleeping bag. Celestial pattern fabric is used for the bag cover with warm, soft fleece for the bag lining. A zipper makes opening the bag easy. Be sure when tucking in your little friends that they've brushed their teeth!

1. To make sleeping bag lining, cut fleece in half to make two 4-3/4" x 10-1/2" pieces.

2. Align top zipper tab with top edge of fleece. Pin edges of fleece along fabric edge of zipper. Stitch down both sides of zipper.

3. With right sides of fabric together, pin open edges of fleece and sew a 1/4" seam down side and across bottom, completing the sleeping bag lining.

4. Make sleeping bag cover by folding cotton fabric with right sides together. Sew 1/4" seam across bottom of fabric.

5. Open zipper on fleece piece. Pin right side of fleece top to right side of cotton fabric. Stitch 1/4" seam across top.

6. Tuck fleece lining inside cotton cover. Fold cover side seams under 1/4". With needle and thread stitch cover closed by sewing cover to zipper fabric.

Materials

9-1/2" x 10-1/2" piece of blue celestial print cotton fabric
9-1/2" x 10-1/2" piece of royal blue fleece
9" zipper
Thread to match fabric
Pins, needle, scissors

Drawstring Bag/Pillow Cover

This little drawstring bag does double duty. It can be used to store the sleeping bag when not in use and it also makes a great pillow cover on which to rest the heads of sleepy bean bag toys. Fill the bag with cotton balls for a quick and easy pillow.

Materials

6" x 8" piece of fabric to match sleeping bag cover
7" length of 1/4" satin ribbon
Pony bead
Thread to match fabric
Small safety pin, iron (optional)

1. Along 8" edge of fabric, fold and sew 3/16" casing. This is the bag top.

2. With right sides together, fold fabric in half to make a rectangle approximately 4" x 5-1/2".

3. Along bottom edge and open side, sew 1/4" seam, stopping at casing stitch line.

4. Pin ribbon to small safety pin and thread through fabric casing.

5. Slip ribbon ends through bead opening. Tie end of ribbon into a knot to keep bead in place.

6. Turn right side out and press if needed.

Chapter 12

Holiday Happiness

The holidays are bright spots in months filled with bleak and dreary days. When Jack Frost nips your nose and arctic blasts of air make it too cold to play outside, you can stay toasty warm inside and pass away the hours playing with your bean bag toys.

Don't forget to include them in your holiday activities. Bean bag toys love to go shopping when ensconced in a backpack. Be sure to bring snack food in case they (or you) get hungry.

If you listen very carefully, you may hear them humming holiday tunes. Just remember, bean bags toys can be very shy. As a result, they only sing when their owners do.

The holidays are about giving, and bean bag toys and accessories make great, inexpensive gifts. There's something special about a gift that's made by hand! Perhaps it's the time, thought, and love that go into creating the gift. Why not consider making some of the projects in this book and giving them as gifts to your extra-special friends or relatives? Just be sure to start projects in plenty of time to avoid adding to holiday stress.

Decorations

Small stockings filled with bean bag toys make great decorations for the tree. Or consider purchasing a small, artificial tree and placing your toys on the tree limbs as decorations. (Be sure not to place toys on limbs of a real tree. Sap from needles and branches can ruin your toys.) A halo of gold garland and angel wings from a craft store can turn any bean bag toy into an angel, but bean bag toys are heavenly with or without wings.

Activities

• Caroling is a wonderful activity for a holiday party. Print song sheets ahead of time to make sure everyone knows the words to the carols. Be sure to dress appropriately for the weather and carry flashlights to light the way and help motorists see you in the dark.

Afterwards, come home and enjoy steaming mugs of hot chocolate served with assorted holiday cookies.

• Spend an afternoon making cookies with friends. Refrigerator cookies, such as sugar, gingerbread, or pinwheel, are perfect for this. To save time and speed clean-up, make the dough the night before and refrigerate. Decorate, if desired, with colored sugar, jimmies, or other decorations.

• Christmas cards are lots of fun to make and receive. Enclose photos of yourself and your favorite bean bag toys in cards you design using construction paper, paint, gift wrap, old Christmas cards, and other materials found around the house.

• Make quick and easy gift bags using brown paper lunch bags. Cut gingerbread men and women out of brown construction paper and decorate with markers and small white rickrack. Glue onto bag with craft glue. Or, make Christmas trees from green construction paper triangles. Decorate with markers or construction paper circles and glue onto bag.

Food

Gingerbread cookies make wonderful tree ornaments and you'll enjoy making them as much as you'll enjoy eating them. Don't limit yourself to traditional gingerbread men and women. Try cookies in animal and other shapes. Make dough following the recipe below and roll and cut out cookies. Before baking, use a bamboo skewer to poke a 1/4" hole in each cookie. After baking, decorate cookies with royal icing (consult a recipe book for royal icing information and recipes), raisins, cinnamon candies, or other favorites. Then thread a piece of ribbon through the hole, tie into a bow, and hang the finished cookie on the tree.

Ingredients

(Makes approx. 6-1/2 cups dough)
1 cup good-quality all-vegetable shortening
1 cup sugar
1 tsp. baking powder
1 tsp. salt
1 cup unsulphered molasses
1 tsp. ground ginger
1 tsp. cinnamon
5 cups flour
4 Tbs. water

Night Before Gingerbread Dough

1. Mix the first seven ingredients on medium speed until well blended.

2. Switch mixer to low speed and add flour and water; continue to mix until dough forms.

3. Roll out dough and cut out with cookie cutters.

4. Bake at 350° for 8 to 10 minutes.

5. Cool cookies on rack. Decorate with royal icing when cool.

Recipe courtesy Nonnie Cargas, derived from her book Gingerbread Houses: Baking and Building Memories. *Krause Publications, 1999.*

Stockings

You'll be sure to hang your stocking by the chimney with care when a bean bag toy can be found peering out from inside. Stockings stuffed with bean bag toys make great holiday decorations. Try hanging them from the mantle, a wreath, or from garland adorning banisters and doorways.

1. With right sides together, fold fabric in half to create 8" x 8" square.

2. Pin stocking pattern to fabric and cut out.

3. With right sides together, stitch a 1/4" seam along sides, heel, and toe, leaving top of stocking open.

4. To finish top opening of stocking, fold fabric over 1/4" and pin in place. Topstitch along edge of stocking opening.

5. Carefully clip heel and toe curves with scissors.

6. Turn stocking right side out and press.

7. Hand stitch lace pieces to stocking body with matching thread. Stitch layers of narrow lace trim along top edge.

8. To make ribbon circles shown on ivory stocking, cut the 18" piece of 1-1/2" lace into three 6" pieces. With needle and thread, sew basting stitch along edge of ribbon. Pull thread, turning flat ribbon into circle. Stitch ribbon circle shut.

Materials

8" x 16" rectangle of fabric (burgundy and forest green velveteen and ivory moiré satin were used here)
Lace pieces
18" piece of 1-1/2" lace
Thread to match fabric and lace
Pins, scissors, needle, iron

Stocking
Cut 1 on doubled fabric

Chapter 13

Miscellaneous Furniture

Sometimes your bean bag toys need a place to hang out as they wait for you to play with them. Small furniture is great for this purpose. Whether it's a rocker, a tuffet, or another piece of furniture, your bean bag toys will love having special pieces created just for them.

Rocking Chair

Materials

"Lil Rock-A-Bit"
Rocker by Mixed
Nuts (see
Resources)
Assorted acrylic
paint
Plastic plate
Artist sponges
Spray acrylic sealer
(optional)

Psychedelic patterned bean bag toys were the inspiration for this sponge painted chair. The chair can also be stenciled or painted a solid color.

1. Assemble rocker according to manufacturer's directions.

2. Squeeze acrylic paint onto plastic plate.

3. Load paint onto sponge by dipping into several colors of paint (Fig. 1).

4. Decorate chair by dabbing loaded sponge onto surface.

5. Wash sponge, squeeze dry, and reload with paint as needed.

6. Allow to dry for 24 hours. Spray with acrylic sealer if desired.

Fig. 1

Tuffet

Little Miss Muffett isn't the only one who likes to sit on a tuffet. Our frog friend gazes longingly into the distance atop a blue velvet tuffet. Perhaps he's thinking about how much more he'd like to eat the spider than curds and whey!

1. Place Styrofoam ball on flat surface.

2. With hand on top of ball, press down and flatten top (Fig. 1).

3. Turn over and flatten bottom (Fig. 2).

4. Place fabric face down on cutting surface. Place plate in center of fabric square. Cut around plate with scissors (Fig. 3).

Materials

4" Styrofoam ball
14" x 14" square blue crushed velvet
12" plate
1/2 yard of 2" tassel trim
Thread
Scissors, needle, glue gun

Fig. 1

Fig. 2

5. With needle and thread, sew basting stitch along edge of fabric circle. Gather fabric by pulling thread. Leave gathers loose enough to insert flattened ball (Fig. 4).

6. Insert flattened ball into gathered fabric. Pull thread to close opening and stitch shut (Fig. 5).

7. Glue trim to top edge with glue gun (Fig. 6).

Fig. 6

Fig. 5

Fig. 4

Fig. 3

Glossary

BASTING STITCHES: Large running stitches.

BODICE: The portion of an outfit between the waist and neck.

CASING: A tunnel of fabric made by turning under the raw edge and stitching along the fabric fold. It is used to enclose elastic or ribbon.

CIRCUMFERENCE: The measurement around the outside of a circular object.

CLIP: A small cut made with scissors.

CORRUGATED PAPER: Paper which has been manufactured with ridges or grooves.

FRAY: To come apart or unravel.

FRINGE: Ornamentation made by cutting narrow slits in fabric at regular intervals.

GATHERS: A row or rows of running stitches or loose machine stitches where thread is pulled to create a ruffle.

HEM: Method of finishing the bottom edge of a garment by turning under the fabric and then stitching by hand or machine.

JUMP RING: A small wire circle used in jewelry making.

LATH: A narrow piece of wood.

PIVOT: A sharp turn made by raising the sewing machine foot while the needle is still in the fabric, rotating the fabric.

PONY BEAD: A plastic bead approximately 1/4" in diameter.

PLEATS: Evenly-spaced folds of fabric which are stitched to hold in place.

RAFFIA: A grass-like material made from palm trees.

RIGHT SIDE: The printed or textured side of fabric.

ROPE ELASTIC: Elastic which is round rather than flat.

RUNNING STITCH: A row of stitches approximately the same size made with a needle and thread or machine.

SNAKE: A tube or coil.

TRIM: To cut away excess.

WAIST: The center of the torso located between the neck and legs.

WRONG SIDE: The plain or untextured side of fabric.

Resources

The supplies used in the projects in this book came from the following companies. Please check the websites listed or your local phone directory for stores in your area.

HOBBY LOBBY STORES, INC.
7707 SW 44th St.
Oklahoma City, OK 73179-4808
Website: www.hobbylobby.com

HOME DEPOT
Website: www.homedepot.com

JOANN FABRICS AND CRAFTS
5555 Darrow Rd.
Hudson, OH 44236-4011
Website: www.joann.com

MICHAELS STORES, INC.
8000 Bent Branch Dr.
Irving, TX 75063-6023
Website: www.michaels.com

MIXED NUTS
221 Rayon Drive
Old Hickory, TN 37138
Website: www.kraftables.com
Manufacturer of "Lil Rock-A-Bit" Rocking Chair